Welcome

introduction

Having produced more than 500 guidebooks and maps to the world's travel destinations, Insight Guides' editors could hardly be expected to ignore what was happening around their own offices in London's Borough High Street. North Southwark, the long neglected district on the south bank of the Thames where Shakespeare first staged his greatest plays and Dickens mined the material for many of his novels, has been vigorously regenerating itself in the era of Queen Elizabeth II as the popular entertainments centre it had been during the reign of the first Elizabeth.

The earliest project to attract international interest was the building of a working replica of Shakespeare's Globe close to the site where the original theatre had stood in the 16th century. Then an aquarium appeared in the former stately home of London's local government, a bleak traffic roundabout sprouted a giant IMAX cinema, and a disused power station was transformed into Tate Modern, a mammoth museum of modern and contemporary art. The world's biggest observation wheel, by Westminster Bridge, changed London's skyline and, in 2000, the Millennium Bridge, the first new river crossing in central London for more than a century, enabled pedestrians to stroll from St Paul's Cathedral to Tate Modern in just seven minutes.

This guidebook, which combines the interests and enthusiasms of two of the world's best-known information providers – Insight Guides,who have set the standard for visual travel guides since 1970, and Discovery Channel, the world's premier source of non-fiction television programming – covers all these attractions and the many others between Westminster Bridge and Tower Bridge. But do not confine yourself to the routes we suggest: much of the joy of exploring this part of London lies in stumbling across unexpected traces of the city's 20 centuries of history in the labyrinth of lanes and alleys. Bear Gardens recalls the popular but cruel sports of Tudor times. King's Head Yard and White Hart Yard evoke the ancient coaching inns that once stood there. Pickwick Street and Copperfield Street summon up the vivid characters that Dickens created to capture the human drama of 19th-century London.

Don't expect a neatly organised 'historic quarter'. Ancient edifices rub shoulders with aggressively modern skyscrapers, elegant Victorian office buildings stand alongside tacky sandwich shops, today's commuters jostle with tourists seeking out yesterday's sites. Southwark is part of a living city, constantly reinventing itself.

Note: Preface London telephone numbers with 020 if dialling from other parts of the UK and with 44 20 if dialling from outside Britain.

Title page: beacon and London Bridge, a 1575 painting by Richard Garth
Preceding pages: Tower Bridge. **Left and Above:** the *Golden Hinde* replica

HISTORY AND CULTURE

London's history began when the Romans built the first bridge across the Thames here. We trace the district's dramatic story through the eras of Chaucer's pilgrims, Shakespeare's players, the British Empire's traders and Dickens's novels to its present-day reincarnation as one of the capital's dynamic entertainment centres...............**9**

ITINERARIES

1 The South Bank runs from Westminster Bridge to Blackfriars Bridge and has a wide range of attractions, including the London Eye, the London Aquarium, the Dalí Universe, the Royal Festival Hall, the National Theatre, the London IMAX Cinema and the Oxo Tower **21**

2 Bankside runs from Blackfriars Bridge to London Bridge and encompasses the massive Tate Modern art gallery, Shakespeare's Globe, the ancient Anchor Inn, Vinopolis: City of Wine, the Clink Exhibition, a replica of Sir Francis Drake's *Golden Hinde*, Southwark Cathedral, Borough Market and the George Inn **37**

3 Pool of London runs from London Bridge to Tower Bridge and includes the London Dungeon, Winston Churchill's Britain at War Experience, *HMS Belfast*, Butlers Wharf and the Design Museum.......................**61**

4 The Imperial War Museum, a world-class institution, deserves an itinerary all to itself. It chronicles the horrors of modern warfare with a variety of hardware and graphic audio-visual exhibits of both world wars. A major new section is dedicated to the Holocaust...................**71**

RESTAURANTS

New restaurants are springing up like mushrooms in this part of London. We pick the best bets **77**

PUBS AND BARS

The most interesting drinking dens in a district with a tradition of hospitality going back 10 centuries...........**84**

PRACTICAL INFORMATION

All the basic travel information and telephone numbers you'll need, with a list of recommended hotels...........**93**

MAPS

Left: detail from William Hogarth's *Southwark Fair*, painted in 1733

History
& Culture

T he Romans chose their site well. In AD43, recognising that the river would be the key to any settlement's strategic importance, they built a bridge across it, using the gravel islands in the marsh that would become Southwark to create a southern approach road for their invading troops. The route remains today, now known as Borough High Street and defended by traffic wardens scarcely less feared than Roman centurions.

Although sharp flints unearthed by archaeologists suggest that humans have inhabited the Southwark area for at least 8,000 years, the increasing tendency of the Thames to flood had turned much of the land into a swamp by the time the Romans arrived, and encouraged them to concentrate the critical parts of their colony on the river's more solid northern bank. But excavations have shown that a substantial suburb was established around the southern approaches to the bridge. In a Roman well unearthed in the crypt below Southwark Cathedral in 1977, archaeologists found discarded sculptures, including a stone hunter-god and a marble dolphin.

Market of the World

Roman Londinium, which derived its name from the Celtic 'Llyn-din' (the fort by the lake), grew rapidly until AD60, when it was attacked and largely burned by guerrillas led by Boudicca (Boadicea), a fearsome red-haired tribal queen who was attempting to drive the Romans out of Britain. Undeterred, the Romans rebuilt the settlement, which by AD100 had supplanted Colchester as Britain's military and trading capital. Around its timber bridge, quays and warehouses had sprung up. Roads radiated to other important centres such as Colchester, York, Chester, Exeter, Bath and Canterbury.

In 410, threatened by the Germanic races from the north, Rome recalled its garrison from England. London's culture withered and its buildings crumbled. It gradually recovered its importance under the Saxons and by the early 8th century was attracting so many traders from abroad that the Venerable Bede, a literary monk, called it the 'Market of the World'. South of the original wooden London Bridge, 'the Borough' was an area granted to London's citizens in 1327 by Edward III; it derived its name from the word 'burgh', meaning fortification, but never in fact achieved the formal legal status of a borough, which would have enabled it to elect its own mayor. Confusingly, the Borough today is only a tiny part of the sprawling borough of Southwark.

Left: detail from *London from Southwark*, painted around 1630 by an unknown artist
Right: many decorative Roman mosaics have been unearthed during construction work

After the Conquest

The bedrock of London's future power was established after the Norman Conquest of England in 1066. William I laid the foundations of what would become the Tower of London, and by 1176 work had begun on a stone London Bridge, wide enough for houses to be built on it. The *Domesday Book*, William's comprehensive survey of his new kingdom, mentions a large church (probably the precursor of the later Priory of St Mary Overie, located on the site of today's Southwark Cathedral) and at least 40 substantial houses, many belonging to Norman lords.

From the 15th century, Bankside gained notoriety as a den of vice. Inns and brothels proliferated, and an unconsecrated graveyard was set aside for prostitutes. The brothels, stretching half a mile along Bankside, drew their customers from the burgeoning city across the river, which increasingly saw the district as a place for entertainment. Southwark, being in the county of Surrey and not part of London, was able to cock a snook at the capital's puritanical legislators, and criminals could take refuge here, outside the jurisdiction of the city's authorities. In 1550 this anarchy was slightly curtailed when the City bought several parcels of land in Southwark from the Crown and designated them a legislative district outside the city walls: 'The Bridge Ward Without'. Even so, some alleys, known as 'liberties', remained outside the city's jurisdiction and continued to harbour murderers and highwaymen.

The entertainment industry resisted suppression too. The annual Southwark Fair, which lasted for up to two weeks each September and continued until 1762, featured freak shows, puppet shows and musicians. Some of London's first playhouses were created here when the authorities banned plays in

Above: the first stone London Bridge, begun in 1176
Right: William Shakespeare, part-owner of the Globe

London proper because they were not respectable activities. Four theatres vied for business on Bankside: the Rose, the Swan, the Hope and the Globe – the latter owned by the King's Men, a group of actors that included William Shakespeare. Bear-baiting and bull-baiting were staged on Bankside from the mid-16th century until the sports were outlawed in 1835. The diarist Samuel Pepys took his wife to a display in 1666 and reported that he saw 'some good sport of the bulls tossing the dogs, one into the very boxes.' But he judged it 'a very rude and nasty pleasure', as did the other celebrated diarist John Evelyn, who declared in 1670 that he was 'heartily weary of the rude and dirty pastime.'

God and Mammon

The 17th century was a time of turmoil for the Church, and several new Protestant sects founded their first meeting-houses in Southwark. John Bunyan drew a crowd of 1,500 when he preached here in 1687, and many religious dissidents were guests in Bankside's Clink Prison before being executed. The *Mayflower*, which carried the Pilgrim Fathers to the New World in 1620, sailed to Plymouth from Rotherhithe (a couple of miles to the east of Tower Bridge), where its captain and many of its crew lived.

Meanwhile, businesses continued to flourish. Merchants, organising themselves into wealthy guilds, had bargained a degree of self-government from subsequent impoverished monarchs and had erected impressive 'gild' halls to the north of the river in what would develop into the City of London, one of the world's great financial centres. Some of that wealth flowed across the Thames, as the historian John Stow reported in 1598: 'The Borough of Southwark… consisteth of divers streets, ways and winding lanes, all full of buildings. As a subsidy to the king, this borough yieldeth about… eight hundred pounds, which is more than any one city in England payeth, except London.'

The oldest surviving view of the city confirms this report. Anthonis van den Wyngaerde's *Panorama of London*, dating from around 1544, shows some fine buildings lining Borough High Street. They include the palatial home of Charles Brandon, Duke of Suffolk, which Henry VIII later turned into a mint. Southwark Cathedral, then the Priory of St Mary Overie, is recognisable, as is St George the Martyr Church, whose square tower has since been replaced by a spire.

But the grandeur was underpinned by widespread poverty. Dutch and German immigrants, who weren't accepted by the City's guilds, plied their trades in Southwark, and many were employed in leather working or brewing – businesses whose pollution made them unacceptable in the City. Such immigrants helped swell Southwark's population from 10,000 in 1547 to 30,000 in 1678. The City fathers also found it convenient to export their criminals and religious dissenters south of the river, and Southwark contained five squalid prisons.

Above: the brutality of bear-baiting, outlawed in 1835

The Age of the Inns

Until 1750 London Bridge was the capital's sole river crossing, and anyone approaching London from the south had to pass through Borough High Street. To cater for this traffic, inns sprang up along the street, offering food and accommodation as well as ale. Many had courtyards where carts and coaches too wide to cross the narrow bridge could be left while their occu-

pants walked to the City of London to conduct their business.

Pilgrims journeying to Canterbury would set off from the Tabard Inn, mentioned by Chaucer in his *Canterbury Tales*. Like most of the area's inns, the Tabard was rebuilt in 1676 after a fire ravaged Southwark; it was finally demolished in the 1870s. The only historic galleried inn to have partially survived is The George *(see page 57)*, also rebuilt after the fire.

By the 18th century, regular stagecoaches were departing from the inns several times a day for all parts of southern England. The inns were the precursors of London's railway stations, which would supplant them. In 1837, when the inns were at their peak, Charles Dickens described them in *The Pickwick Papers*: 'Great, rambling, queer, old places they are, with galleries, and passages, and staircases, wide enough and antiquated enough to furnish material for a hundred ghost stories.'

The 1676 fire destroyed many venerable buildings in Borough High Street as well as the Tabard. Planners struck in 1830, sweeping away most of the remaining old structures on the west side in order to widen the street and realign London Bridge. Today, the only remaining half-timbered house with an overhanging upper floor can be glimpsed down an alley at No. 50.

Ordeal by Fire

Fire had long been a threat in London. As early as the 11th century, William the Conqueror had imposed a curfew – his *couvre-feu* – which compelled citizens to douse all fires at nightfall. In the early 13th century a devastating fire engulfed London Bridge, which supported many wooden houses, trapping

sightseers and firefighters. According to the historian John Stow: 'Then came there to aid them many ships and vessels into which the multitude so inadvisedly rushed that, through fire and shipwreck, three thousand people were killed.'

In 1633 a servant left hot ashes under a flight of stairs on the bridge, causing a fire that destroyed half the structure. Ironically, the gap left in the bridge's houses prevented the Great Fire of London spreading across to Southwark in 1666. But 10 years later a blaze wiped out much of the east side of what is now Borough High Street, destroying many of the old inns.

Brick buildings lessened the impact of fires, but didn't prevent them. Insurance companies developed fire insurance policies and found it cost-effective to hire Thames watermen to extinguish fires in buildings under their cover. The trouble was that, if a brigade employed by an individual insurance company turned up at a burning building not insured by its particular employer, it would leave the fire to rage. It wasn't until 1833 that various brigades banded together to form the London Fire Engine Establishment, with 80 full-time firefighters. But their resources weren't great enough to save the Houses of Parliament, much of which burnt down in 1834, or to contain a fire in a riverside warehouse in Tooley Street, close to London Bridge, in 1861, which raged for two days and smouldered for another two weeks. As a result, the government agreed to set up a publicly funded city-wide fire brigade.

The Industrial Revolution

As overseas trade expanded, warehouses began appearing downstream from London Bridge. The Hay's Wharf Company, whose name is carried on by Hay's Galleria *(see page 63)* today, was founded in 1651. A century later, the building of new bridges – Westminster in 1750, Blackfriars in 1769 – spurred economic growth, and the Industrial Revolution provided the technology to drain much of Southwark's marshy land and generated the capital to build factories and houses on that land. The area had long attracted craftsmen – the legendary Southwark School of Glaziers produced some of the country's most renowned stained glass in its St Thomas Street works from 1515 to 1531 – but the new working methods emphasised machines more than skills. Gas production, a vinegar works, a steam-powered corn mill and London's largest brewery were among the top employers.

Brewing encouraged the hop trade to gravitate to Bankside; the scale of the trade can be judged by the magnificent 1866 Hop Exchange on Southwark Street *(see page 55)*. Many locals, unable to afford holidays, spent a month each year picking hops on farms in Kent – back-breaking work but at least a change of scene. By the end of the 19th century iron foundries, engineering works and small printers had all congregated in Southwark. The silk hat trade employed 1,500.

Top left: the Tabard Inn in the 17th century
Bottom left: the Tooley Street fire of 1861
Right: glass-blowing was a local industry

The Healing Tradition

In 1726 Thomas Guy, a boatman's son who had made a fortune from shrewd investments, founded Guy's Hospital, across the road from the overstretched St Thomas' Hospital. Later benefactors included Britain's first car tycoon, Lord Nuffield, founder of Morris Motors, whose statue stands in the hospital's inner courtyard. The poet John Keats (1795–1821) was a medical student at Guy's, which grew into one of London's most important teaching hospitals; today it has a 30-storey tower and beds for 1,000 patients.

Its neighbour, St Thomas', had been founded in the 12th century by the Priory of St Mary Overie. It pioneered modern nursing and was where Florence Nightingale set up her training school after the Crimean War. In 1862, due to be demolished along with the homes of 8,000 people to make way for an extension of the railway from London Bridge to Charing Cross, the hospital relocated to Lambeth, on the south side of Westminster Bridge, and today includes a Florence Nightingale Museum.

The names of other institutions tell much about social conditions at the time: the Magdalen Hospital for Penitent Prostitutes, founded in 1768, and the Philanthropic Society to Protect the Needs of the Abandoned Children of Criminals (1788). As slums proliferated in the 19th century – one Tooley Street house, for example, packed 41 people from eight families into eight rooms – the Metropolitan Association for Improving the Dwellings of the Industrial Classes began to provide tenement buildings. There were few controls on small factories and a parish magazine described graphically how 'all disagreeable smelling trades were carried on in the neighbourhood, haddock smokers, bone-boilers, horse slaughterers.' The insanitary conditions led to frequent

Above: Bethlem Hospital, now the Imperial War Museum
Right: Charles Dickens, chronicler of Southwark's low life

outbreaks of cholera and other diseases. Four children in 10 died before their fifth birthday.

It was not until 1849 that a clear link was established between disease and contaminated water – even Florence Nightingale thought epidemics were air-borne – by which time the stench from the Thames, virtually an open sewer, was great enough to drive Members of Parliament from the Chamber of the House of Commons. The 'Great Stink' of 1858 created the political will to finance a proper sewage system for London and encouraged central government to involve itself in social reform, previously seen as the responsibility of local authorities and the Church. The novels of Charles Dickens played a crucial role in drawing the attention of middle-class Victorians to the plight of the lower classes in areas such as Southwark. Various official boards and charitable institutions were set up to provide food and fuel for the needy and to build schools, but increasingly the capital needed an overall body to tackle its problems in a coordinated way. In 1889 the London County Council was created and Southwark, which had remained part of the county of Surrey, officially became part of London.

Song and Dance

For all the poverty, Southwark was still a centre for entertainment. Many of the huge number of pubs – about one for every 500 people – employed singers and musicians, and out of these grew the music halls. In an area that today hosts the Ministry of Sound's massive dance club, halls such as the 4,000-seater South London Palace of Varieties sprang up, attracting top performers such as Marie Lloyd and Dan Leno. Charlie Chaplin was a local boy, born into a music hall family.

The area's population peaked at 131,000 in 1901 – nearly three times what it is today – and then began a gradual decline as improved transport and the provision of cheap public housing in the new suburbs enabled many to escape

the slums. Manufacturing industry and the docks still employed most people, usually on a casual shift basis. More than half the nation's butter and cheese, imported from New Zealand and Australia, passed through the Hay's Wharf Company in Tooley Street. The economic activity was impressive – so much so that the docks were a major bombing target for zeppelins during World War I.

The expansion of the docks in the 1920s was reversed by the economic depression of the 1930s, but housing conditions improved for many people, thanks mainly to the London County Council's ambitious building programme. The LCC also made a big investment in schools.

Right: detail from Walter H. Lambert's *The Stars of the Edwardian Music Hall* (1901–3)

World War II

The docks were a major target during the blitz, a traumatic period vividly depicted in today's Imperial War Museum *(see page 72)*. Because Southwark was built on marshy ground, it was hard to provide underground bomb shelters that wouldn't flood. Many people took shelter by night under railway

arches, but these offered little protection if hit during a raid. More than 2,500 civilians in Southwark were killed between 1940 and 1945.

The post-war building boom replaced much of the housing stock, although the slab-like tenement blocks provided scant visual pleasure. Factories benefited from rebuilt premises, but their initial recovery was short-lived. In the 1960s company takeovers made many of the small industrial units redundant and the docks were served with a death sentence as international freight transferred to mighty container ships unable to use the small, unmechanised berths in Southwark.

The dockers saw a further threat to their jobs as immigrants began to settle in the borough. Their resistance was bitter but futile: around a third of today's population belongs to an ethnic minority. In 1983, Sam King, who had been one of the first 492 immigrants from Trinidad and Jamaica to arrive at Tilbury Docks on the *Empire Windrush* in 1948, became Southwark's first black mayor.

Regeneration

By the 1970s, much of Bankside consisted of cheap warehouses and was hard to reach by public transport – although it did attract film companies intent on shooting Victorian costume drama. In the 1980s the focus was on improving the South Bank to the west and on creating a massive new business district in Docklands to the east. Some artists and designers moved to Bankside, lured by the cheap rents, but for most people an evening visit to the Anchor or George inns was an exotic outing, requiring a detailed map. A couple of newspapers, also attracted by the lower rents, forced their journalists to cross the river (just) – the *Financial Times* moving to the southern end of Southwark Bridge and Express Newspapers to the southern end of Blackfriars Bridge. But it was the campaign of actor-director Sam Wanamaker (1919–93) to build a replica of Shakespeare's Globe *(see page 42)* that first drew the attention of most Londoners to the forgotten area. The real turning point came in 1994 when the Tate Gallery decided on the disused Bankside Power Station as a home for its international modern art collection.

By the time Tate Modern opened in 2000, connected to the northern bank of the Thames by the svelte Millennium footbridge, Bankside was hailed as one of the city's coolest areas. London Bridge Station was planning a £400 million redevelopment, creating a new complex of shops and offices. Borough Market had begun selling its fresh produce to health-conscious consumers under the revived 19th-century slogan 'London's Larder'. Waterloo had

Above: clearing up after a World War II bombing raid on Southwark

swept the homeless from the concrete bunker in front of the mainline station, replacing them with an eye-catching IMAX cinema. County Hall, the former seat of London's local government, had been reborn as a hotel and entertainment complex *(see page 21)*, overlooked by the world's biggest observation wheel. Costly plans were laid to prettify the South Bank Centre and to regenerate the run-down Elephant and Castle shopping centre. An Eco-bus was planned to propel tourists between the attractions using liquefied petroleum gas.

As final confirmation that the once disreputable district where Shakespeare and Marlowe had plied their trade was being formally integrated with the rest of London, the Underground arrived. The 10-mile (16-km) extension to the Jubilee Line connected London Bridge Station directly with both Docklands and the West End. One of the six new stations built was Southwark, situated at the junction of Blackfriars Road and The Cut. Like the other new stations, the spacious design had a stylish finish not seen since the classic Underground stations of the 1930s. Tellingly, architects had been involved at an early stage, working alongside engineers, instead of being brought in at the end 'to put the lipstick on the gorilla', as had been the practice with more recent Underground lines.

It was the juxtaposition of old and new that gave the quarter its excitement. Futuristic buildings began to take shape round the corner from the atmospheric alleys that once led to the old coaching inns. Smart youth-oriented bars shared the same street with shabby old pubs. Trendy bakers offered an alternative to the unimaginative sandwich shops.

The Shock of the New

But along with the vibrancy came a certain alarm. Could the exciting mix of old and new survive or would the characterful old buildings be replaced by a skyline of skyscrapers? Would the artists' studios be turned into loft apartments for bankers? Even as the old power station regenerated itself as Tate Modern, local residents were organising resistance to a proposal to drive a new railway line across the river from London Bridge to Blackfriars, obliterating the old shops and housing that lay in its path. The articulate, monied newcomers expressed their views, as did the existing working-class residents. The fight for Southwark's soul is unending.

Above: London Bridge's Jubilee Line Underground station
Right: the Southwark Needle at the end of London Bridge

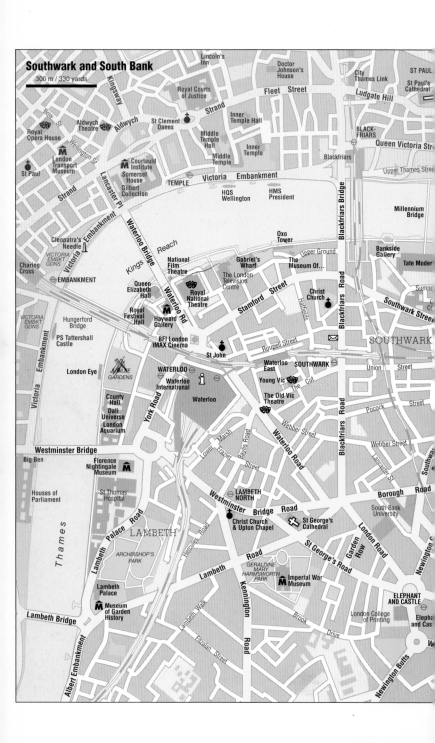

Southwark and South Bank

300 m / 330 yards

Lincoln's Inn
Royal Courts of Justice
Kingsway
Doctor Johnson's House
City Thames Link
ST PAUL
St Paul's Cathedral
Fleet Street
Ludgate Hill
Strand
St Clement Danes
Inner Temple Hall
BLACK-FRIARS
Queen Victoria Str
Bow St
Aldwych Theatre
Aldwych
Middle Temple Hall
Inner Temple
Blackfriars
Upper Thames Street
Royal Opera House
Wellington St
London Transport Museum
Middle Temple
Millennium Bridge
St Paul
Courtauld Institute
Somerset House
Gilbert Collection
TEMPLE
Victoria Embankment
HQS Wellington
HMS President
Blackfriars Bridge
Strand
Lancaster Pl
Waterloo Bridge
Reach
Oxo Tower
Bankside Gallery
Tate Moder
Cleopatra's Needle
Victoria Embankment
Kings
Upper Ground
The Museum Of...
Charing Cross
VICTORIA EMBKT GDNS
National Film Theatre
Gabriel's Wharf
The London Television Centre
Christ Church
EMBANKMENT
Queen Elizabeth Hall
Waterloo Rd
Royal National Theatre
Stamford Street
Hatfields
Southwark Stree
VICTORIA EMBKT GDNS
Hungerford Bridge
Royal Festival Hall
Hayward Gallery
Roupell Street
SOUTHWARK
PS Tattershall Castle
BFI London IMAX Cinema
St John
Waterloo East
SOUTHWARK
Union
Street
London Eye
JUBILEE GARDENS
WATERLOO
Waterloo International
Young Vic
The Cut
Pocock
Street
County Hall
Waterloo
The Old Vic Theatre
Dali Universe
London Aquarium
Webber Street
Webber Street
Westminster Bridge
Lower Marsh
Baylis Road
Frazier Street
Waterloo Road
Lancaster St
Southwa
Big Ben
Florence Nightingale Museum
LAMBETH NORTH
Borough
Road
Houses of Parliament
St Thomas' Hospital
Westminster
Bridge
Road
South Bank University
London Road
Thames
Lambeth Palace Road
LAMBETH
Christ Church & Upton Chapel
St George's Cathedral
Garden Row
Newington C
ARCHBISHOP'S PARK
Road
St George's Road
Hercules Road
GERALDINE MARY HARMSWORTH PARK
Lambeth Palace
Lambeth
Imperial War Museum
ELEPHANT AND CASTLE
Lambeth Bridge
Museum of Garden History
Kennington
Road
London College of Printing
Elepha and Cas
Albert Embankment
Lambeth Walk
Fitzalan Street
Brook
Drive
Newington Butts
W

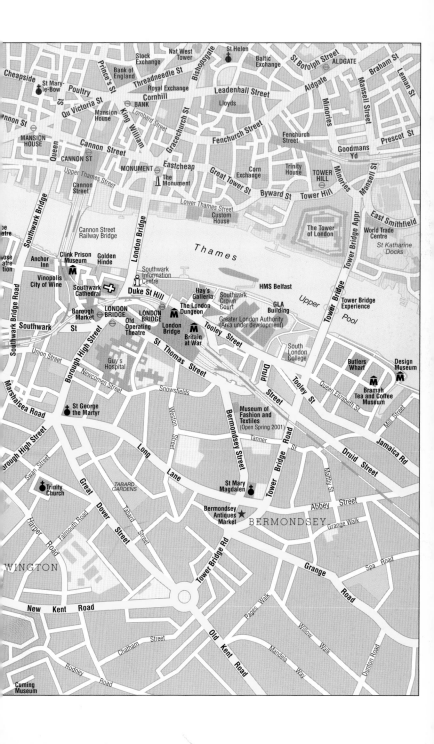

The
South Bank

1. WESTMINSTER BRIDGE TO BLACKFRIARS BRIDGE

Westminster Bridge

Linking County Hall, the former seat of London's local government, with the Houses of Parliament, Westminster Bridge – made from cast iron and consisting of seven graceful arches – was built between 1854 and 1862, replacing an earlier bridge built in stone in the 1740s. At one time eight trams every minute in each direction passed over Westminster Bridge, but today it is less busy than its neighbouring river crossings. Among the bridge's many literary connections, the most memorable is William Wordsworth's poem *On Westminster Bridge*:

> *Dull would he be of soul who could pass by*
> *A sight so touching in its majesty*

The imposing statue of Queen Boudicca (Boadicea) in her chariot on the north side of the bridge is by Thomas Thornycroft; she was the warrior who tried to drive the Romans from Britain in the 1st century AD. The Coade Stone Lion by W. F. Woodington at the southern end of the bridge is originally from the entrance to the now defunct Lion Brewery (the secret of how to make Coade Stone, a type of terracotta, has now been lost).

County Hall

This imposing building, designed in Edwardian Renaissance style, was built between 1909 and 1922 – World War I interrupted progress – as the headquarters of the London County Council. When the LCC's successor, the Greater London Council, was abolished by Margaret Thatcher's government in 1986 (its policies being too left-wing for the Iron Lady to stomach), London was left without an overall governing body and a new use had to be found for the grand building facing the Houses of Parliament across the river. That new purpose proved elusive and Japan's Shirayama Shokusan Corporation, which bought it for £60 million, ended up dividing it between an upmarket hotel (Marriott), a utilitarian hotel (Travel Inn), an aquarium, a gallery devoted to Salvador Dalí and several unmajestic attractions such as a games arcade and a branch of McDonald's.

It seemed that Mrs Thatcher's humiliation of the Greater London Council was complete, but in 2000 the last leader of the abolished council, Ken Livingstone, had his revenge when he was elected as London's first city-wide mayor. An imposing headquarters for the new body he chairs, the Greater London Authority, began taking shape near London Bridge (*see page 61*).

Left: the London Eye
Right: the Coade Stone Lion

London Aquarium

If aquariums conjure up memories of rainy childhood holidays at the seaside, where dusty rooms with a few murky tanks were marginally more exciting than the local lifeboat museum, prepare to be dazzled and delighted by County Hall's central attraction, the **London Aquarium** (daily 10am–6pm, last admission 5pm, closed Christmas Day; admission charge, tel: 7967 8000). A gently descending route, ideal for wheelchairs and pushchairs, winds through seven different aquatic environments on three levels, beginning with freshwater stream, voyaging through the world's great oceans and ending with coral reefs, rainforest and mangrove swamps. Thousands of specimens representing 350 species of fish inhabit over 440,000 gallons (2 million litres) of mains-fed but specially treated water. Atmospheric sounds, smells and lighting have been employed to great effect: dragonflies hum around the freshwater stream, tropical birds call in the steamy rainforest, the air has a salty tang at 'Beach Pier'.

Slicing through two floors of the complex are two giant 25-ft (7.6-metre) high cylinders representing the Atlantic and Pacific oceans, the latter patrolled by three different types of shark that weave through models of the monolithic statues found at Easter Island. Ledges allow spectators to sit within a window's-breadth of these mean-looking creatures; the windows are made of

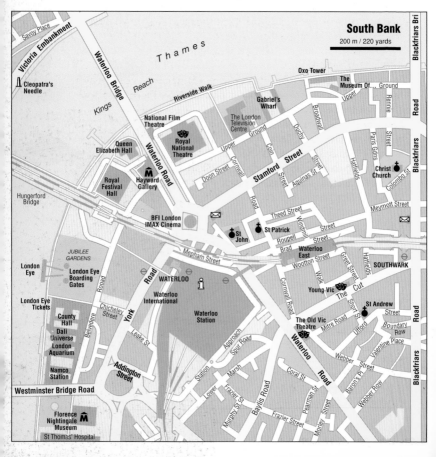

acrylic and are 17 times stronger than ordinary glass.

Fish are a great source of fascinating facts, and there is a huge amount of background information at one's fingertips through interactive and audio-visual displays, but it can be more mind-expanding to wander and gaze at random, marvelling at the ugliness of the dogface puffer fish, the hypnotic beauty of a tank full of mauve-coloured jellyfish, or the amazing African lungfish, the only fish to have developed its own set of lungs – for use in the dry season when it is surrounded by mud. Popular with children are the 'Beach Pier', where cleverly camouflaged rays (apparently related to the shark) waft to the surface to be tickled by eager fingers, and the 'Rock Pool' where members of staff help in the handling of starfish, anemones, crabs and suchlike.

It is worth catching the special shark and rainforest talks (tel: 7967 8029 for schedule) and feed times (shark feeding Tues, Thurs, Sat 2.30pm; piranha feeding, in Tropical Freshwater, Mon, Wed, Fri and Sun 1pm), when divers deliver a mix of mackerel and squid. Sharks are surprisingly modest eaters, consuming about 12 mackerel each a week.

Namco Station

To the right of the Aquarium entrance as you face Country Hall, **Namco Station** is an interactive neon-lit entertainment centre for children of all ages with loud ear-bashing music and hypnotic flashing lights, and a collection of games that would put any self-respecting arcade to shame. Not only is it home to the latest Playstation and video games, but there are also bumper cars, a bowling alley and fantastic simulators including Grand Prix motor racing and jet-skiing. For visitors who pine for Las Vegas or Monte Carlo, there's a selection of fruit machines (off-limits to anyone under 18). Visitors use special Namco currency, a token called a Nam – this is worth 50 pence and can be purchased inside the complex.

Refreshments are on sale and there is a licensed bar which also serves snacks. The centre is open every day 10am–midnight and there's a DJ at weekends. Tel: 7967 1067; website: www.namco.co.uk. Entrance is free.

Above and right: the London Aquarium

The Dalí Universe

Given some of the political rows that shook County Hall when it was the centre of London's government, the blend of surrealism and self-publicity perfected by Salvador Dalí (1904–89) would have fitted in seamlessly. The **Dalí Universe** (daily 10am–5.30pm; admission charge; tel: 7620 2420), which takes up 30,000 sq ft (2,800 sq metres) of the building, puts more than 500 of his works on show. Its entrance is to the left of the Aquarium as you face the building, and its presence is promoted by three riverside sculptures: *Space Venus*, *Space Elephant* and *Nobility of Time* (these aren't unique – Dalí normally made his sculptures in editions of 12).

Curated by Benjamin Levi, an Italian art dealer who knew the artist and

collects his work, the exhibition is divided into three themed areas: 'Sensuality and Femininity' (which includes the well-known Mae West Lips Sofa and the sculpture *Buste de Femme Retrospectif*), 'Religion and Mythology' (which includes St George and the Dragon and the epic illustration of Dante's *Divine Comedy*), and 'Dreams and Fantasy' (which includes *Persistence of Memory* and *Profile of Time*). Especially notable is the collection of 124 drawings that Dalí produced to accompany his 1942 autobiography *La Vie Secrète*. 'Like all surrealists,' says Levi, 'he wanted to create something that didn't have any sense by combining two things that on their own were quite sensible.'

Dalí has always divided critics, but fans prepared to pay the high ticket prices will find much of interest here, and the exhibition complements the wider collection of surrealist work at Tate Modern, further along the river.

London Eye

Towering over County Hall is the British Airways-sponsored **London Eye**, the world's largest observation wheel. Hyde Park was considered as a location for this millennial project, but it ended up here by the Thames at Jubilee Gardens. Some critics complained that it impinged unhappily on the classic lines of the former seat of London's government, but that didn't deter the public. When the Eye opened in early 2000, it became an instant money-spinner, and the Tussaud's Group, which handles the ground arrangements, found itself coping with even longer queues than those customary at its Marylebone Road waxworks. Ticket touts endorsed the wheel's success by offering £7.45 tickets to would-be riders at up to £20.

The statistics alone impress. At 450 ft (135 metres), it is the fourth highest structure in London. The hub and spindle weigh 330 tonnes – heavier than 40 double-decker buses. The 32 fully enclosed capsules, each holding 25 people, take 30 minutes to make a full rotation – a speed slow enough to allow passengers to step in and out of the capsules while the wheel keeps moving. On a clear day, you can see for 25 miles (40 km).

Above: Benjamin Levi, founder of the Dalí Universe
Top right: Dalí's *Space Elephant*. **Right:** the view from the London Eye

The idea of building a giant Ferris wheel to celebrate the turning of the millennium came from architects David Marks and Julia Barfield in 1995. For much of the next few years, they fought to stop the essence of their innovative design being diluted to save money. One idea – that the wheel be driven by the flow of the Thames – had to be jettisoned because the tides weren't powerful enough. However, the essential concept – the elegant pods and the wheel supported on one side only, like a giant desktop fan – survived.

By the time planning permission and financing had been obtained, it was a race against time to build the wheel, and contracts were spread across Europe. The observation capsules were made in France, their curved glass panels in Venice, and the 75-ft (23-metre) steel spindle in the Czech Republic (by Skoda). After the components had been brought up the river by barge, the wheel was assembled in a horizontal position on temporary platforms anchored to the riverbed before being pulled gingerly over several days into its vertical position.

So stately is the rotation that there is no feeling of movement inside the capsules. A solid floor keeps vertigo at bay and a central bench is provided in each capsule in case anyone feels dizzy. There's a security guard in each capsule, primed to provide information about the 'flight' and to identify landmarks.

But is the experience worth queueing for? A well-travelled Californian in our capsule rated it '6 out of 10, perhaps 7' and that's probably about right. Londoners will enjoy spotting familiar buildings, but visitors may be left with an impression of an incoherent urban sprawl with only a few

sights – the Houses of Parliament, Buckingham Palace, the Dome at Greenwich – immediately identifiable. The enduring impressions are that London is a surprisingly low-rise city, that it has quite a lot of green space and that it is resolutely unplanned.

Planning ahead is desirable if you hope to ride the London Eye at busy periods, though. You can make an automated telephone booking on 0870 5000 600 (but check the weather forecast first if possible). If you prefer to turn up and queue, do so early in the day; even then, a ticket you buy mid-morning may not entitle you to a ride until mid-afternoon.

The South Bank concert halls

Along the river to the east of Jubilee Gardens, a small park now dominated by the London Eye and displaying a copy of *The Profile of Time*, Dalí's dripping clock, is the **Royal Festival Hall** (RFH), the oldest and largest of the three concert halls on the South Bank. Built on the site of the Lion Brewery, destroyed by bombing during World War II, it was opened in 1951 as part of the Festival of Britain, a celebration designed to improve the country's morale after five years of post-war austerity.

The architects of this grade I listed building, Robert Matthew and Leslie Roberts, paid great attention to the hall's acoustic design, with the intention that the sound should carry uniformly around the auditorium, whether full or empty. Even so, the acoustics are not to every conductor's taste. Large cavity walls insulate the audience and performers from outside noise, and the stage can be raised and lowered to provide a space for dance and opera, as well as symphonic concerts.

In 1967 the 2,900-seat RFH gained two smaller neighbours, the **Queen Elizabeth Hall** and the **Purcell Room**. The QEH seats 917 people and is designed for chamber concerts, music theatre and opera. The 372-seater Purcell Room is intended for solo recitals and chamber music.

The RFH is currently the home of the Philharmonia Orchestra (principal conductor Christoph von Dohnânyi) and the London Philharmonic (principal conductor Kurt Masur). The Orchestra of the Age of Enlightenment is the hall's associate orchestra. Performances by the contemporary music ensemble, the London Sinfonietta, and of Opera Factory, noted for their radical productions, take place at the QEH.

Two other ensembles resident at the South Bank are the Alban Berg Quartet and the New London Consort. The South Bank also takes part in an annual jazz festival, puts on concerts of world musics, and also has its own gamelan (a percussion-dominated Javanese orchestra).

The policy of maintaining an 'open foyer' opens the halls' cafés and bars, and

Left: the South Bank Centre in foreground, with the Royal National Theatre middle right

book and record shops to the public throughout the day. The foyer of the RFH is also used as an exhibition space for sculpture, photography and painting, and is the venue for free concerts (12.30–2pm daily; Commuter Jazz early Fri evenings). August sees the foyer used for the annual Ballroom Blitz dance festival. In addition to bars and cafés, the RFH also has the People's Palace restaurant, with great views of the river *(see page 77)*. Plans have recently been put forward for a huge redevelopment and refurbishment of the South Bank site. Proposals include a new concert hall (possibly to replace the QEH), improvements to the acoustics of the RFH and development of the foyer and riverfront areas.

Booking for all concerts can be made by phone (tel: 7960 4242 from 9am–9pm Mon–Sat, 9.30am–9pm Sun) or at the RFH in person 10am–9pm daily, and the QEH and Purcell Room 45 minutes before performances. Listings for future South Bank Centre concerts can be found online at www.sbc.org.uk, where online bookings can also be made.

Hayward Gallery

Tucked away in the South Bank Centre's brutalist concrete jungle between the Royal Festival Hall and the National Theatre is the **Hayward Gallery** (daily 10am–6pm, until 8pm Tues and Wed; admission charge but concessions available; tel: 7960 4242). Opened in 1968, the Hayward is one of Britain's most important and versatile art spaces for temporary modern-art exhibitions. It is also responsible for the extensive loan collection of the Arts

Council, which is used to bring modern British art (such as works by Francis Bacon and Henry Moore) and contemporary British work (recent acquisitions include pieces by Damien Hirst and Gillian Wearing) to a wide public. The Hayward also organises touring exhibitions, which reach around 160 venues across Britain.

The Hayward's cutting-edge programme focuses on four areas: single artists (from Renoir, Dalí and Bonnard to Bridget Riley, Jasper Johns, James Turrell and Antony Gormley); historical themes and artistic movements (such as Art and Power: Europe under the Dictators 1930–45); other cultures (recent exhibitions have explored the art of ancient Mexico and the first Australians), and contemporary themes (notably shows on art and film and on sound). You can contact the Hayward's box office *(see number above)* or visit the gallery's comprehensive website (www.hayward-gallery.org.uk) for details of what's currently on show. Exhibitions tend to be busy towards the beginning of a run – a tip is to visit early on Sunday morning, when it's usually quieter – and it's advisable to allow at least a couple of hours to make your way around the multi-level space. Note that on Wednesdays (4.30–7.30pm) and Sundays (1–4pm), artists are on hand to answer your questions.

Above: the Royal Festival Hall, dwarfed by the Shell Centre office block

If you're inspired by the work on show and want to buy art-related merchandise, the gallery's shop is just off the front foyer. If you need a rest halfway, there's a café, refurbished in 1999, upstairs. Before you leave, look out for the funky Neon Tower on the roof of the gallery. Commissioned in 1970 from Philip Vaughan and Roger Dainton for a Kinetics exhibition, this London landmark is composed of yellow, magenta, red, green and blue neon strips, which are controlled by changes in the direction and velocity of the wind.

Waterloo Bridge

Waterloo Bridge, which soars over the riverside walkway at this point, has inspired countless painters, writers and lyricists – improbable as this may seem during gridlocked rush-hours. *Waterloo Bridge*, a Hollywood weepie about a ballerina who turns to prostitution after hearing that the soldier she loves has been killed, was made three times – in 1931, in 1940 and (retitled *Gaby*) in 1956 – and a classic Kinks track, *Waterloo Sunset*, captured a very 1960s mood. In good weather, and especially after dark, a stroll across the bridge provides stunning views of the river and its waterside architecture.

The first bridge at this point, known as the Strand Bridge during its six-year construction, was built by John Rennie and described at its opening in 1817 as 'the noblest bridge in the world, worth a visit from the remotest corner of the earth.' But in 1923 its piers began to settle ignobly into the Thames mud and it was demolished, amid protests, in 1936. The present-day cantilevered structure by architect Sir Giles Gilbert

Above: secondhand bookstalls by the riverside
Left: there's usually an ice-cream van close by

Scott (designer of the classic red telephone kiosk and the power station now housing Tate Modern) was built between 1939 and 1942, much of it by female labour after the menfolk went off the war. Waterloo Bridge was also the scene of a famous unsolved crime when, in 1978, a Bulgarian dissident was killed by a stab from the tip of a poisoned umbrella while making his way home across the river.

BFI London IMAX Cinema

If you're a fan of the big screen, you may at this point wish to leave the riverside walk and cut up the approach road to Waterloo Bridge, just to the south of the Hayward Gallery. This brings you to the elevated roundabout at the southern end of Waterloo Bridge. Until 1997 the space below this roundabout was a windswept concrete wasteland occupied by dozens of homeless people who slept in cardboard boxes and kept warm in winter by lighting fires around the pillars supporting the bleak walkways linking Waterloo Station with the South Bank. Then a remarkable transformation occurred as the down-and-outs were rendered even more homeless by the erection of a spectacular glass rotunda housing Britain's biggest cinema screen.

The London IMAX Cinema (tel: 7902 1234) is part of the British Film Institute which, more skilful in seeking handouts than the residents of Cardboard City had ever been, received £15 million of national lottery money towards the cost of the £20 million building. Its shape echoes that of the Globe Theatre and the bearpits that provided popular entertainment south of the Thames four centuries earlier, but it is emphatically a child of modern technology. The 5,000-tonne, 482-seater cinema rests on 60 giant springs designed to eradicate vibration from Waterloo & City tube trains running just 15 ft (4.5 metres) beneath it. Large-format film – 10 times the size of standard 35mm stock – is projected onto a screen 66 ft high by 85 ft wide (20 by 26 metres). The 11,600-watt digital surround-sound system, deploying 44 speakers, is ideal for experiencing the sensation of a space shuttle blasting off from Cape Canaveral.

The first generation of IMAX films has favoured natural history, blending the spectacular with the educational in scenes featuring underwater explorers, mountaineers and astronauts. Most last 40 to 50 minutes, and many are made in a 3-D format, viewed through spectacles that cost £36 (US$55) to make and are far more effective than the cheap red-and-green plastic versions of the 1950s. How well the IMAX format can handle compelling narrative remains to be seen, but it has an attractive novelty value and fits comfortably into the South Bank entertainment mix.

Right: London's largest screen

The National Film Theatre

Back by the Thames, nestling almost invisibly beneath the southern end of Waterloo Bridge, is a more conventional type of cinematic experience: the **National Film Theatre**, Britain's leading arthouse cinema (box office: 7928 3232 11.30am–8.30pm). It opened in 1952, taking over from the Telekinema, whose 3-D exhibits at the Festival of Britain were one of its most popular features. Far from the mass-market glitz of Leicester Square with its giant multiplex cinemas, the NFT has followed its mission to attract cinema-goers to higher levels of the art-form (although this hasn't prevented the occasional screening of TV-serial favourites such as *The Avengers* and *Dr Who*).

With three auditoria, the NFT holds more than 2,400 screenings and events each year, from lovingly restored silent movies (to a live piano accompaniment) to pioneering world cinema productions, to the latest Hollywood blockbuster. Controversial films have often been shown here, including *The Wild One* (with Marlon Brando in motorbike gang battles) and more recently David Cronenberg's *Crash*, a disturbing fusion of sex and car smashes. You can become an NFT member to obtain special benefits and discounts.

The NFT's biggest annual highlight is the London Film Festival, in November, which presents hundreds of films from around the world, including major gala premieres. Every April the London Lesbian and Gay Film Festival, established as one of the foremost events of its kind, is held at the NFT. Also of note are the Guardian Interviews at the National Film Theatre. Started in 1980, these regular events have hosted many of cinema's most famous names, including Bernardo Bertolucci, Sir Richard Attenborough, Quentin Tarantino, Spike Lee and Whoopi Goldberg.

In about 2003, the National Film Theatre is scheduled to move premises again, this time to a riverside film centre to be built between the Shell Centre and the British Airways London Eye. The new building will also be home to the British Film Institute and a regenerated Museum of the Moving Image (until recently one of the South Bank's most innovative attractions). Meanwhile, taking advantage of the shelter provided by Waterloo Bridge, a number of secondhand booksellers have set up their stalls outside the NFT, offering a varied selection of titles with a distinct bias towards the arts.

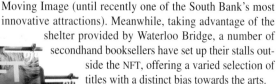

The Royal National Theatre

The next riverside edifice in the South Bank Centre's relentless concrete jungle is the **Royal National Theatre** (box office: 7452 3000; information: 7452 3400; website: www.nt-online.org). It has no seasons as such; old and new plays are presented in repertoire all year. The turn-around is fast – up to nine productions in any two weeks – and the venue draws big-name actors and directors. Shakespeare and Stoppard, Molière and Tennessee Williams are

Above: cinema icons at the National Film Theatre

staged alongside extravagant musicals, new plays and visiting productions, and the main criticism of the programming is that European theatre, both classical and contemporary, is inadequately represented.

The idea of a National Theatre was first suggested in 1848, but repeated attempts to get the scheme off the ground were unsuccessful. It wasn't until 1912, when Lilian Baylis became manager of the Old Vic Theatre on Waterloo Road (*see page 71*), that the basis for a National Theatre was established. She turned the old Victorian music hall into 'the home of Shakespeare and opera in English'. But finding a suitable site for a permanent theatre proved difficult, and foundation stones were abortively laid on four separate occasions. During World War II, the government introduced funding for the arts as part of the war effort, the London County Council made land available on the South Bank, and in 1949 the National Theatre Bill was finally passed through Parliament unopposed. Laurence (later Lord) Olivier was named artistic director in 1962 and founded the first National Theatre Company.

The Old Vic remained the company's home for 13 years, while the new theatre was being built, with Denys Lasdun the appointed architect. In 1976, after more than a century of struggle and controversy, the National Theatre was opened by the Queen, by which time Peter Hall was at the directing helm. He was succeeded by Richard Eyre in 1988, the year the National was granted its 'Royal' title to mark the company's 25th anniversary (and perhaps to aid fund-raising a little). The current director, Trevor Nunn, who made his reputation with the Royal Shakespeare Company and his fortune by directing Andrew Lloyd-Webber musicals, was appointed in 1997.

The South Bank complex houses three theatres under one roof. The **Olivier**, which seats up to 1,200 people, is the biggest. The design of the fan-shaped auditorium is based on the Greek amphitheatre at Epidaurus and the stage is a set designer's dream. It has a revolving drum with elevators that can bring scenery and props smoothly on and off the stage

Above: a Christmas outing for *Peter Pan* at the Royal National Theatre

during performances. The **Lyttelton** is a more conventional two-tier proscenium theatre, with room for about 900 people. The smallest and most intimate of the trio is the **Cottesloe**, a rectangular room with a floor space surrounded by galleries on three sides, where both seating and stage can be rearranged to suit the play. This space is often used for more experimental theatre.

Lasdun called the **foyer** (Mon–Sat 10am–11pm) the 'fourth auditorium', with the London skyline, visible through the floor-to-ceiling windows, as the backdrop. It's a lively social centre open to everyone, with free exhibitions and live music, early evening events and a bookshop. There are plenty of people-watching spots with bars and cafés dotted across all floors and outdoor terraces overlooking the river. If you are coming to see a performance, interval drinks and sandwiches can be ordered in advance from all the theatre bars and, if you really want to push the boat out, the Olivier has its own 'modern British' restaurant at mezzanine level *(see page 77)*.

For a fascinating peek behind the scenes, book yourself onto a backstage tour (Mon–Sat at 10.15am, 12.30pm – or 12.15pm on Olivier matinee days – and 5.15pm; fee; reservation advisable 7452 3400). Each tour lasts about an hour and takes you through the three auditoria, the scenic workshops, corridors strewn with props and bits of scenery, and the organised chaos of the wings. Two practical tips: a space in the car park below the National costs £5.70 after 5pm, and bicycle racks can be found outside the Espresso Bar on the corner of Theatre Square.

Gabriel's Wharf

Immediately to the east of the National Theatre is an IBM office building and, beyond it, an 18-storey tower housing **London Weekend Television**. Founded in 1968 and now owned by the Granada group, LWT has the franchise for broadcasting ITV programmes to the London area from Friday evenings until the early hours of Monday morning. Its prestigious arts programme, *The South Bank Show*, takes its name from the location. The public can attend recordings of shows such as *Blind Date* in the London Studios, part of the LWT complex (for details, tel: 7261 3261).

Gabriel's Wharf, a small group of single-storey buildings backed by a striking set of *trompe l'œil* paintings, was created as a temporary site in the late 1980s and is part of Coin Street Community Builders, a non-profit company created to improve the South Bank as a place to live, work and visit. Eventually the site will be used to provide affordable new housing. The area contains a selection of speciality shops, studios and restaurants *(see page 78)* around an open space dotted with seating and wood carvings. It is one of the main platforms of the Coin Street

Above: a National Theatre performance of Maxim Gorky's 1904 *Summerfolk*

Festival, London's principal free arts festival, held every summer. Visitors can find snacks and meals at the various venues around the square, and bicycles can be hired from the London Bicycle Tour Company (tel: 7928 6838), which also organises guided sightseeing tours of London. Imaginative hand-

crafted jewellery and gifts are offered at several different studios and offbeat shops sell textiles and imported artefacts from around the world. The Skylark Art Gallery is run by 14 exhibiting artists offering a variety of styles at, they claim, exceptionally low prices. Fashion designers, milliners and print makers are all represented. The Wharf is a pleasant place to sit and watch the world go by before continuing a stroll along the river.

Oxo Tower territory

One of the South Bank's best-known landmarks, the Art Deco **Oxo Tower** (tel: 7401 2255; www.oxotower.co.uk) is a reminder that local campaigning *can* make a difference. In the 1980s, redevelopment of the riverfront called for the tower to be demolished and a huge modern construction put in its place. The dwindling number of local residents (down to just 4,000 from 50,000) banded together to form the Coin Street Action Group, thereby saving the tower and its pale purple lights which have twinkled out at Londoners since the late 1920s.

The distinctive 'O-X-O' design on the Art Deco building came about because its owners, the Liebig Extract of Meat Company, made a stock cube called Oxo, which is still in production today). Architect Albert Moore had grand ideas: as well as erecting what was to become London's second highest commercial building, he wanted to use electric lights to spell out the product's name. When planning permission was refused, Moore came back with 'an elemental geometric form' using three letters: O, X, and O as 10-ft (3-metre) high windows looking out north, south, east and west. The ploy succeeded.

Today, the site is a pleasant blend of commercial and residential space, and the 78 low-rent flats for people in need of housing are in great demand (applicants outnumber properties 40 to 1). On the river side is the Coin Street information centre, where books and brochures can be found. Almost next door is **the.gallery@oxo** (free), an art space with a mix of changing exhibits. Upstairs are two storeys of small retail/design spaces,

Right: eating out at Gabriel's Wharf

specialising in contemporary work. The shops (open 11am–6pm, closed Mon) double as working studios, so you can watch a piece being made or commission one there and then. The range of artists and goods is sweeping: from Doreen Gittens' gossamer-light wedding fabrics to Richard Hinton's witty, structural lights.

Unfortunately, with so many entry points and a sterile lift area in the middle, the Oxo Tower can be difficult to get to grips with, especially if you're trying to find the public viewing gallery. Not only do signs along the way cease to exist, but the gallery is smack in the middle of the haughty Oxo Tower Restaurant (*see page 78*), which does little to help.

Here's how to get there: take the lift to the eighth floor. Exit and turn left, towards the *restaurant* (not the brasserie or the bar). Turn left again and walk smartly through a glass corridor lined with Harvey Nichols products. Don't be intimidated by the stylish media people wolfing down *châteaubriand au poivre* on all sides, but do be aware that, as most of the terrace is reserved for the restaurant, the public area is small, so try to avoid lunch times. The intrepid will be rewarded with a lovely view of the river, the Inns of Court and Blackfriars Bridge. As the gallery is open in the summer months until 10pm, you could also arrive at sunset or later – particularly pleasant on a soft warm night when the rhythmic strains from a salsa barge come drifting up from across the water.

Immediately to the south of the Oxo Tower, located in an unconverted warehouse on the site of Henry VII's Royal Bargehouse, is **The Museum Of...** Its incomplete name indicates that it constantly changes its focus, holding temporary exhibitions (on subjects such as 'Me' and 'The Unknown') that challenge preconceptions of the traditional 'look, don't touch' museum. Not only do the artists invade the space (e.g. by painting the walls), but

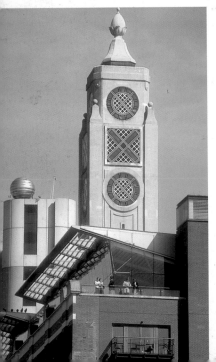

the public are also invited to contribute to the works of art. You will experience sound, smell, touch and the satisfaction of leaving your own mark, as well as enjoying other people's reactions to the exhibits. It's amazing how an empty warehouse can be so versatile depending on the layout and colour of the show installed. It can be a bit cold, though, so wear something warm. The Museum Of... will hold a temporary exhibition on 'The Unknown' before installing a permanent Museum of the River Thames in 2001.

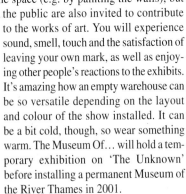

On the riverside walk just before Blackfriars Bridge, the large block adorned with golden nautical carvings is owned by the Sea Containers shipping group. It was originally designed as an upscale hotel, but the South Bank was not then the tourist draw it is today, and most of the building was converted into apartments.

Left: the self-promoting Oxo Tower
Right: St Paul's from Blackfriars Bridge

b a n k s i d e

Bankside

2. BLACKFRIARS BRIDGE TO LONDON BRIDGE

Blackfriars Bridge

Officially known as the William Pitt Bridge, Blackfriars Bridge was the third bridge to be built across the Thames. The name Blackfriars derives from a black-robed medieval Dominican order whose monastery once stood on the north side of the river. The original bridge was built between 1760 and 1766, replaced between 1865 and 1869, and widened between 1907 and 1909. The present bridge was designed by architects Cubitt and Carr and features five cast-iron arches. In a grizzly incident in 1982, the body of an Italian banker, Roberto Calvi, was found hanging beneath the bridge and subsequent conspiracy theories stretched all the way to the Vatican. Historical scenes of the Thames, carved in stone, decorate the pedestrian underpass on the Thames Path on the south side of the river.

The office block to the east of the bridge proclaims itself as **Express Newspapers** and is what remains of the extensive newspaper empire built up by the freebooting Canadian publisher and politician Max Aitken, later Lord Beaverbrook. Despite countless changes of editors and formats in the past 30 years, the circulations of the middle-market *Daily Express* and *Sunday Express* have continued to slide, and the group is now part of United News & Media, whose main focus has shifted to its television interests.

As you continue eastwards, look out for the unobtrusive **Bankside Gallery** (Tues 10am–8pm, Wed–Fri 10am–5pm, Sat–Sun 1–5pm; admission charge; tel: 7928 7521). It is home to the Royal Watercolour Society and the Royal Society of Painter-Printmakers, which broke away from the Royal Academy in an attempt to raise the profile of the neglected art forms of watercolour painting, and etching, engraving and mezzotint work. The gallery hosts regular exhibitions of members' work throughout the year, each lasting 5–6 weeks. All exhibited work is by living artists and the programme is varied and accessible. Artists' prints can be bought at the adjoining Gallery Book Shop. The Gallery has a rich collection of archive material relating to works on paper, viewable by appointment. There are regular opportunities, usually on Tuesday evenings, to meet featured artists for an informal discussion and viewing.

Left: a remnant of an old railway bridge close to the modern Blackfriars Bridge (**right**)

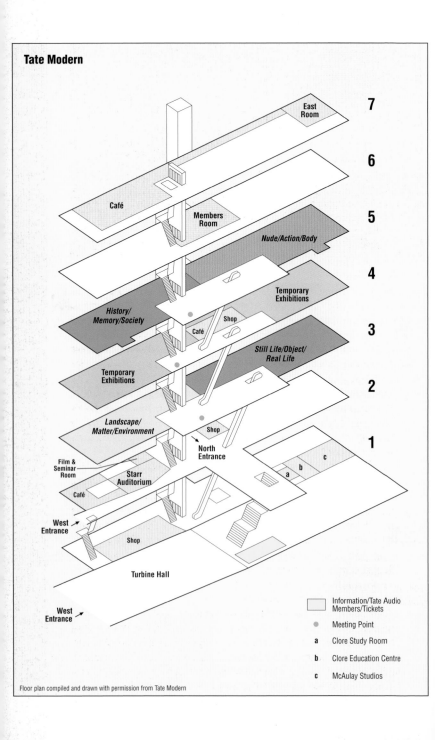

Tate Modern

7 East Room

6

5 Café | Members Room | Nude/Action/Body

4 History/Memory/Society | Temporary Exhibitions

3 Café | Shop | Still Life/Object/Real Life

2 Temporary Exhibitions | Landscape/Matter/Environment | Shop

1 North Entrance | Film & Seminar Room | Starr Auditorium | Café | a | b | c

West Entrance | Shop

Turbine Hall

West Entrance

Information/Tate Audio Members/Tickets
● Meeting Point
a Clore Study Room
b Clore Education Centre
c McAulay Studios

Floor plan compiled and drawn with permission from Tate Modern

Tate Modern

The Bankside Gallery must have felt like a Thames tug-boat nudged by an ocean liner when its massive next-door neighbour, **Tate Modern**, opened to the public in May 2000. Turning over its old gallery on the other side of the Thames at Millbank to its collection of British art from 1500 onwards, the Tate boldly moved its entire international modern collection and part of its contemporary collection, most of which had been kept in storage for lack of space, to the converted Bankside Power Station.

This vast brick edifice competes for attention with the remarkable contents of its 88 galleries, which range from Picasso's *Weeping Woman* and Dalí's *Lobster Telephone* to the very latest works of international artists. Given the unexpected setting, it's appropriate that Surrealism has a conspicuous presence in Tate Modern.

The building, which is remarkable if not a thing of beauty to every eye, was originally designed by the architect Sir Giles Gilbert Scott (1880–1960), whose other creations include Battersea Power Station and Waterloo Bridge *(see page 28)*. Measuring more than 650 ft (200 metres) in length along its riverside front and incorporating 4.2 million bricks, it was built in two phases. Work on the western part, including the 325-ft (99-metre) high chimney, began in 1947, and the power station began to pump out oil-fired fuel in 1953. The extension at the eastern end was added in 1963. But Bankside's working life was short: by 1981 it could no longer compete with cheap fuel imports and was declared redundant.

The new role for the turbine-driven dinosaur was revealed in 1994, when the Tate bought it for £11 million and appointed the Swiss firm of Herzog & de Meuron to transform it. Their stylish £134 million conversion maintains the integrity of the original design, while creating a space fit to house one of the world's most notable modern-art collections. As a humorous aside, they have added a small, ordinary-looking fireplace to the interior to complement the building's gigantic chimney.

Above: Tate Modern

Admission to Tate Modern (Sun–Thurs 10am–6pm, Fri–Sat 10am–10pm, galleries open at 10.15am; tel: 7887 8008) is free. If you approach it from St Paul's by walking across the Millennium Bridge, you will enter the gallery on its north side. The main entrance, however, is on Holland Street, to the west of the building. This takes you into the ground floor through a broad sweep of glass doors and then down a massive concrete ramp. The impressive space in front of you, covering more than 35,000 sq. ft (3,300 sq. metres) and rising six storeys, is the Turbine Hall, the old boiler room. Now devoid of its power-generating machinery, the hall is both a throughway – a wide, lofty corridor through the heart of the building, which is described by Tate Modern as a 'covered street' – and a gallery capable of housing massive sculptural works and installations.

This is 'one of the great spaces for modern art,' says Sir Nicholas Serota, the Tate's director. Natural light floods in through Herzog & de Meuron's principal new design feature – a two-storey glass roof or 'lightbeam' that runs the entire length of the building.

Each year until 2004, with Unilever sponsorship, Tate Modern will commission a large-scale artwork that will enjoy pride of place in the Turbine Hall. The 2000 exhibit, a mighty installation by the French-American sculptor Louise Bourgeois, was constructed from three 30-ft (9-metre) high steel towers, entitled *I Do*, *I Undo* and *I Redo*, each one topped by a platform surrounded by a series of mirrors (visitors with heads for heights can reach them via spiral staircases up the towers). Bourgeois' showpiece aims to create a place for reflection and intimate encounters and is a spectacle in itself. It also provides an excellent vantage point from

Above: Tate's Turbine Hall
Right: Louise Bourgeois' spider

bankside

which to appreciate the enormity of the Turbine Hall, though arachnophobes will not be able to take their eyes off Bourgeois' menacing metal spider.

Along the north side of the Turbine Hall are the main rooms of the gallery, which can be accessed by several escalators, staircases and lifts. The permanent collection, including work by Picasso, Matisse, Mondrian, Duchamp, Dalí, Bacon, Pollock, Rothko and Warhol, plus sculpture by Giacometti, Hepworth and Epstein, is housed on the third and fifth levels. Works are organised in four

themes – the nude, landscape, still life and history painting. There are two themes per level, each shown in a suite of galleries, and each suite would easily merit a visit on its own. Displays are multi-disciplinary, enabling installations, sculptural works and photography to be interspersed among the paintings.

Although this thematic system of display has been criticised by those who prefer a more traditional chronological system of hanging, Tate Modern's curators argue that the themes chosen are 'classic' ones, rooted in genres originally established by the French Academy. The intention is that the juxtaposition of work produced before the 1970s (an imprecise dividing point) with the work of contemporary artists will help visitors to understand how artists have learnt from one another since 1900.

Level four provides a home for temporary exhibitions (note that an entrance fee is charged for these). The inaugural show, entitled 'Between Cinema and a Hard Place', featured work by artists including Christian

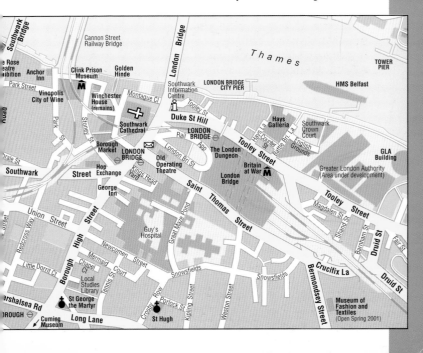

Boltanski, Rebecca Horn, Anish Kapoor, Bruce Nauman, Cornelia Parker and Rachel Whiteread.

A second-level café has fine views across the river and the top-floor café, housed in the lightbeam, has even better ones *(see page 80)*. Other facilities include a 240-seat auditorium decorated in a heady blood-red – the vivid walls, ceiling, floor and furnishings coming as a surprise after the minimalism of the main galleries. There's also a screening room, offices, and a splendid balconied room for members. Visitors with mobility impairments can park next to the gallery if they book in advance by telephoning 7887 8008.

The Millennium Bridge

Linking one of London's oldest tourist attractions, St Paul's Cathedral on the north side of the Thames, with one of its newest, Tate Modern on the south bank, the innovative Millennium Bridge became in 2000 the first new river crossing in central London since Tower Bridge opened in 1894. It takes about seven minutes to walk between the two buildings, and the views are captivating.

Designing the footbridge was a tricky assignment: it had to be slender and unobtrusive enough so as not to spoil the view of St Paul's from Bankside, yet it had also to make an impact as a significant millennial sculpture. The solution, a sort of stainless-steel scalpel, was provided by a triumvirate consisting of architect Lord (Norman) Foster, sculptor Sir Anthony Caro and engineers Ove Arup and Partners. 'We wanted a platform, a flying carpet that is as thin as possible,' said Arup's Roger Risdill-Smith. Using horizontal suspension cables enhanced the thinness. However, opening-day crowds caused the bridge to sway excessively, and it was closed temporarily for an engineering rethink.

Shakespeare's Globe

Continue to walk eastwards along the Thames and you reach **Cardinal's Wharf**. In 1502, Catherine of Aragon, who was to become the first of

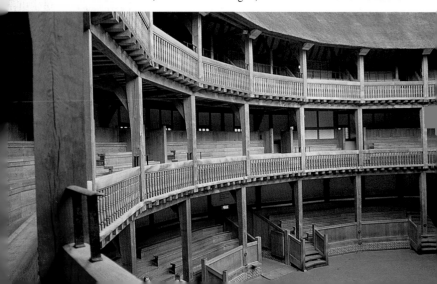

Henry VIII's six wives, took shelter in one of the houses here when she first landed in London. A plaque on the house also states that Sir Christopher Wren lived here for a time while his masterpiece, St Paul's Cathedral, was being built on the other side of the river between 1675 and 1710 – but historians say this claim is completely bogus.

Shakespeare's Globe, to the left of Cardinal's Wharf, is unapologetically bogus. It is a re-creation, completed in 1997, which is both smaller than the Tudor original and some distance from the original's location. But the new Globe Theatre is a thriving, vibrant place, and a stunning tribute to the persistence of the American actor-director Sam Wanamaker. He first visited Bankside in 1949, seeking the site of Shakespeare's 'wooden O', but was bitterly disappointed to find nothing more than a dingy plaque attached to the side of a brewery. After founding the Shakespeare Globe Trust in 1970, he began a long battle against British indifference and officialdom and faced a massive task of fund-raising. Eventually he won the battle and, by the time he died in 1993, work on the reconstruction was well advanced.

The first Globe had no easy time either. It was originally known as 'The Theatre' and was situated on the north side of the Thames at Shoreditch, but when the sons of its founder, actor-manager James Burbage, abandoned a

lengthy battle to extend the lease, they hired a master carpenter, Peter Street, to demolish The Theatre and transport the timbers across the Thames during Christmas 1598. William Shakespeare (1564–1616) acted here and was a part-owner. *Hamlet, Othello, King Lear* and *Macbeth* all had their first performances at the Globe. The theatre prospered on Bankside for 14 years until a stray piece of wadding from a stage cannon landed on the roof during a performance of *Henry VIII*, setting fire to the thatch. The audience survived but the Globe didn't. Several months later a lavish new theatre reopened – this time with a tiled roof. But acting remained a suspect activity, and in 1642 Cromwell's Puritans closed the theatre down.

The Globe has been painstakingly re-created using the original methods of construction. All the wood is oak, the roof – open in the centre – is thatched with Norfolk water reed (but specially treated to resist fire), and the joints are all made with wooden pegs. The 36,000 Tudor bricks were handmade and the ingredients of the plaster were also traditional: sand, lime, water and animal hair. The only difference was the type of hair: the 20th-century version used cashmere because modern cattle aren't as hairy as their ancestors.

The season of the open-air galleried theatre runs from May to September, with a professional company of international actors performing Shakespeare and other appropriate plays under artistic director Mark Rylance. His philosophy is based on three As: architecture, audience, actors. The artists are encouraged to interact with the audience. No amplification is used or needed because the acoustics are so good that a whisper can be clearly heard in the

Top left: the Millennium Bridge, connecting St Paul's and Tate Modern
Left: Shakespeare's Globe **Above:** detail from the gates of the Globe

galleries, and only natural lighting is used. The theatre, which is particularly suited to Shakespeare's comedies, can accommodate 1,500 people – 600 standing (and liable to get wet if it rains) and the rest seated. The wooden benches can feel distinctly hard by Act III, but you can rent cushions.

The fascinating Shakespeare's Globe Exhibition, to the right of the theatre, is well worth a visit. Housed in the vast UnderGlobe, it aims to bring aspects of Shakespeare's work vividly to life using a combination of modern technology and traditional crafts. A combined ticket includes a guided tour of the theatre (mornings only on matinee days). The Trust also runs a varied educational programme for students of all ages through its Globe Education Centre in the nearby Bear Gardens, exploring Shakespeare's scripts in relation to the stage for which they were written. The Inigo Jones indoor theatre is due to open in 2001.

Public booking for the theatre opens at the beginning of February and the box office is open Mon–Sat 10am–8pm (6pm when the theatre is closed). Box office tel: 7401 9919, fax: 7902 1475. The Exhibition is open daily, including weekends (except Christmas Eve and Christmas Day) Oct–Apr 10am–5pm, May–Sept 9am–midnight. There's a café, open from 10am, and a restaurant, open from noon *(see page 80)*. Both have good views of the Thames. There's also a gift shop.

The Rose Theatre

Shakespeare also acted at the **Rose Theatre**, whose foundations were discovered close by in 1989. Turn down New Globe Walk (by the Globe's box office) and then left into Park Street, which runs along the back of the Globe complex. At Number 56, the **Rose Exhibition** (open every day except Christmas and Boxing Day, 10am–5pm; bookings and enquiries: 7593 0026, admission charge), a sound-and-light presentation narrated by Sir Ian McKellan, tells the story of the Rose, Bankside's first theatre. Built in 1587 by Philip Henslowe, the theatre, which featured in the Oscar-winning film *Shakespeare in Love*, had a repertory that included plays by Christopher Marlowe. It fell into disuse as other more modern and spacious theatres were built.

The remains were found by archaeologists from the Museum of London carrying out routine checks between the demolition of one building and the construction of its replacement. When it became clear that they had found a site of immense importance, a campaign was launched to save the site from destruction by the building work. The piling for the foundations was moved so that the site could be saved and the remains of the Rose are now housed in a separate basement under the new building. Unfortunately the chalky foundations, which had been protected by the marshy nature of the site, started to dry and crack and have had to be covered in protective layers of sand and cement and flooded with water to protect them until enough money can be raised to re-excavate, conserve and display this historic excavation.

Above: Southwark Bridge; the tower is part of Cannon Street railway station
Right: benches by the Thames outside the Anchor Inn

Southwark Bridge

If you turn left out of the Rose Exhibition and continue along Park Street – where a plaque opposite the back entrance to the *Financial Times* building marks the site of the original Globe Theatre – you reach Vinopolis *(see page 47)*. If, instead, you cut back to the riverside walk, you will pass under **Southwark Bridge**, London's least-used river crossing (around 16,000 vehicles a day). A private company was formed to build the bridge in 1813. It was thought at the time that the bridge, situated at one of the narrowest points of the river, would slow down river traffic but construction went ahead anyway. The bridge, designed by John Rennie, had a single central span of 240 ft (73 metres) which was the world's largest cast for an iron bridge – so large, in fact, that it bankrupted the casting company which made it. That bridge was replaced between 1912 and 1921 by a five-span steel bridge designed by Ernest George.

The large letters FT displayed on the black glass of Number One, Southwark Bridge identify it as the headquarters of the ***Financial Times*** newspaper, which first appeared on 13 February 1888 and turned pink five years later. In 1989, with the advent of new printing technology, the FT quit Bracken House, its previous home near St Paul's Cathedral, and moved south of the Thames to this practical six-storey block. The paper isn't actually printed here – that happens in a Docklands plant and in 14 other cities around the world. The FT dominates financial journalism in the UK and is locked in an international circulation battle with the *Wall Street Journal*.

The Anchor Inn

Most journalists like to have a good pub close by, and the fondness of the *Financial Times* staff for the **Anchor Inn**, the next riverside attraction, persuaded the inn's management to name one room the FT Bar. The Anchor (Park Street, tel: 7407 1577; Mon–Sat 11am–11pm; Sun noon–10.30pm) is no ordinary pub: an inn has stood on this site for 800 years, and the present building, dating to 1770–75, is the sole survivor of the 22 busy inns that once lined Bankside.

A maze of passageways, the Anchor combines a minstrels' gallery, ancient oak beams, dark staircases, creaking floorboards, and hiding holes where escapees from the nearby Clink Prison would take refuge or where drinkers would shelter in the 18th century when persuasive recruiting teams arrived to pressgang patrons into the Navy. Even the ladies' toilets are special, with low ceilings, delightful tiles, faded velvet armchairs and glowing lampshades in the anteroom. The pub contains a collection of objects from the reign of Elizabeth I (1533–1603), found during excavations, and a model of its former neighbour, the original Globe Theatre.

The residents of Southwark reputedly embarked on a pub crawl along Bankside to witness the ferocious Great Fire of London in 1666, coming to rest at the Anchor. The diarist Samuel Pepys, a regular at the tavern, was among the onlookers. Another literary regular was the lexicographer Dr Samuel Johnson, and a capacious chair in the downstairs Johnson Bar is said to be where he scribbled notes for his celebrated *Dictionary of the English Language* (1755), the first of its kind in English. A more recent luminary to prop up the bar was Tom Cruise, seen enjoying a swift pint here in the 1998 movie *Mission Impossible*.

In the 15th and 16th centuries the alehouse on the site was known as the Castle on the Hoop, but later fell derelict. The building assumed its present shape when a Mr W. Allen bought it in 1770 and converted it into a dwelling house with a brewhouse attached. Ale was traditionally produced in the area: Geoffrey Chaucer mentioned the 'ales of Southwark' in his 14th-century *Canterbury Tales*, and the Anchor Brewery continued to operate until 1957. It still serves some of the best tradtional English beers.

A popular riverside terrace has good views of St Paul's and Tower Bridge and there's a walled courtyard for summer barbecues. Upstairs, the dining room provides more views of the river and serves fine English food.

Vinopolis

Across the road from this boldly traditional pub is the main entrance to **Vinopolis, City of Wine** (tel: 0870-4444 777), which takes a very different approach to the pleasures of drinking. Occupying 2½ acres (1 hectare) of old warehouses and cathedral-like spaces under railway arches, this sprawling attraction is an innovative combination of entertainment and education. As well as a strikingly visual wine tour through exhibits of the world's major wine regions, there are shops, restaurants *(see page 81)*, conference facilities and an art gallery.

'I tried to give it a feeling of theatre,' says Duncan Vaughan-Arbuckle, the former wine importer who founded Vinopolis. Set designers from West End musicals were hired to provide themes for the various vaults. The Italian vault, for example, has imposing Roman statuary and arches; it also has five Vespa scooters on which you can sit and, as film is projected onto their windshields, have the illusion that you are driving through Italian vineyards. The South African section has a frontage of an old Dutch colonial house, with a garden containing a variety of (artificial) local plants. The California section has old Hollywood movie cameras. Reproductions of Van Gogh, Renoir, Cézanne and Monet lend atmosphere to the France section, as does a battered Citroën delivery van and a statue of the wine-loving François Rabelais.

The education element is provided by individual audio units and earphones giving access to four hours of recorded commentary in six languages. As you walk into each country area, an introductory commentary – delivered by well-known wine journalists such as Hugh Johnson, Jancis Robinson and Oz Clarke – is automatically triggered. Many individual exhibits display a number that, when keyed into the audio unit, supplies a specialist commentary. The information ranges from details of wine production techniques to interesting titbits (e.g. until as recently as 1990 it was illegal for supermarkets in New Zealand, one of the world's more respected wine producers, to sell the stuff).

The admission fee to the wine tour (£11.50 at time of writing) looks pricey at first but does include tickets for five wine tastings at tables along the route; these offer a choice of more than 200 wines plus the advice of knowledgeable staff. Any of these wines can be bought by the bottle from the Majestic Wine Warehouse store at the end of the tour. An adjacent gift shop claims to stock the world's widest selection of champagne and wine glasses plus accessories (e.g. 43 different corkscrews) and gourmet food (e.g. caviar, chocolates and a huge range of olive oils). Entrance to the shops and restaurants is free if you don't wish to take the tour.

But is the tour worth taking? Yes, if you like wine, want to know more about it, and have time to listen to a reasonable portion of the commentary. Wearing earphones can inhibit sharing the experience with companions, and children (who are denied the fun of the wine tastings) may get fidgety. Last admission to the tour is 3.30pm Tues–Fri and 6pm Sat–Mon.

Left: Duncan Vaughan-Arbuckle, founder of Vinopolis
Right: the exterior of Vinopolis, City of Wine

Clink Exhibition

To the left of Vinopolis's main entrance is Clink Street, whose main attraction is the **Clink Prison Museum** (daily 10am–6pm; fee; tel: 7378 1558), which can be identified by the emaciated figure suspended within a cage from the blackened gable end. Founded perhaps as early as the 12th century to deal with overenthusiastic revellers, the lock-up functioned until 1780, latterly as a debtors' prison, and the word 'clink' became a synonym for jail.

Dimly lit steps lead down into the entrance of the museum, where tacky trinkets and souvenirs, and an interesting short history of the prison, are on sale. You then enter a dismal series of rooms that represent cell interiors while a disembodied voice drones in the background, sentencing various miscreants of the Middle Ages to a range of ever-worsening punishments. Effigies of scrawny inmates are displayed in varying degrees of discomfort.

Beside each exhibit, plaques give information on various aspects of prison life and history; for example, that the Clink was allegedly the first English prison to admit women inmates, mainly prostitutes, for crimes as

benign as 'chiding' their clients. One frightening punishment was to 'gently' pull apart the erring whore by attaching ropes to her limbs, the other ends being fastened to a couple of horses. The cells have replicas of many of the horrific instruments of torture used by the prison wardens; some are truly ingenious. In 1530, Henry VIII ordered a new and particularly gruesome punishment: slow-boiling in oil.

With the Clink being outside the jurisdiction of London in those days, the area swarmed with brothels, bear- and bull-baiting rings, and theatres and taverns – all considered forms of 'suspect' entertainment by the authorities. The prison was never short of inmates – including, among others, monks and priests with views differering from those of the sovereign. On at least one occasion, the entire cast of one of the South Bank theatres was thrown into the Clink for lewd behaviour. This area of Southwark (formerly known as 'the Liberty of the Clink') was under the control of the bishops of Winchester, who ruled by their own laws and founded the Clink Prison. Realising that, if you couldn't eradicate sin, you could at least make money by licensing it, the bishops regulated the brothels; the whores became known as 'Winchester geese'. Following an outbreak of syphilis, Henry VIII (himself a sufferer) closed the brothels in 1546, but by the 17th century they were thriving again.

The bishops' London base, **Winchester Palace**, was just to the east of the Clink Prison Museum. Only a single gable wall (illuminated at night) remains, though an adjacent plot is being excavated.

The Golden Hinde

Clink Street leads on to Pickfords Wharf, built in 1864 for storing hops, flour and seeds, and now an apartment block. At the end of the street, in the **St Mary Overie Dock**, is a full-size replica of Sir Francis Drake's galleon,

Above: the remains of Winchester Palace

the ***Golden Hinde*** (open daily 9am–sunset; admission charge; information 7403 0123, bookings 08700-118700). The Devon-built ship, launched in 1973, toured Britain and North America as a travelling museum until it came to rest here in 1996, and is the only replica to have completed a circumnavigation of the globe. It has thus clocked up more nautical miles than the original, in which Drake set sail in 1577 on the greatest piratical voyage in English history. During his three-year marathon, he allegedly claimed for Queen Elizabeth I the territory now known as California.

Climbing aboard and moving through the replica (minding your head on the ceilings, which are less than 6 ft/2 metres high to keep the ship's centre of gravity low), it's easy to imagine life at sea on such a vessel. Particularly striking are the cramped and harsh conditions endured by the sailors. They spent their lives either at work or asleep on the bare decks, which were often under an inch of water; they had only one set of clothes and no privacy or personal possessions. Answering the call of nature was a hazardous procedure, involving clambering down onto the beakhead at the bow of the ship, and tying yourself to the ship to avoid losing your grip as the beakhead went under water. Diet was poor and many men perished at sea, although Drake was ahead of his time and supplemented their meagre and festering rations with fruit whenever possible. For this reason, survival rates aboard his ships were better than average, which probably helped his recruiting.

In return for committing themselves to this unenviable lifestyle, the sailors would receive a share of the treasure that Drake plundered. The booty was divided up between Queen Elizabeth I, the sponsors of the voyage, Drake himself, the officers (usually second sons of the aristocracy who needed to find themselves an income) and finally the crew, with even the lowliest receiving a substantial sum of money. During his three-year circumnavigation of the globe, Drake accumulated too much booty to fit in the hold, and he had to replace the ballast (the rocks in the bilge that kept the ship stable) with gold. The *Golden Hinde* thus earned the reputation of being the only ship whose ballast was worth more than the vessel itself.

St Mary Overie Dock, which was noted in the *Domesday Book*, William the Conqueror's 1086 property survey, was named after a monastery that stood here until dissolved by Henry VIII in 1534.

Above: the *Golden Hinde*
Right: the ship's carved hinde

Southwark Cathedral

Continuing to the right past St Mary Overie Dock brings you to **Southwark Cathedral** (closed except for worshippers during services; suggested admission charge), on your left. It is one of the great historic buildings of south London, packed with fascinating treasures. Its excellent lunchtime concerts also make it a popular attraction for workers in the area, who can also lunch in the cathedral's restaurant (due to reopen in spring 2001). Services are held: weekdays 8am, 12.30pm and 5.30pm; Saturday 9am, 9.15am and 4pm; Sunday 8.45 am, 11am, 3pm and, first Sunday of the month only, 6.30pm.

Archaeological finds have indicated human activity on the site since around 500BC, and the discovery of a statue of a Roman hunter god (a replica is on display near the altar) during building work in the 1970s suggest that it may have been used for pagan worship prior to the spread of Christianity. Excavations have also revealed the floor of a Roman villa, a section of which is incorporated in the south aisle, and Roman road posts.

According to local legend, the first Christian building on this site was a nunnery founded in the 7th century by Mary, the daughter of a local ferryman called Overie. This was reputedly replaced by a community of priests established by St Swithin, Bishop of Winchester from 852 to 862. But the first documentary evidence of the building's history is found in the *Domesday Book* (1086), which records how a monastery was founded here in the reign of Edward the Confessor (1042–66). In 1106 the building of a new church, St Mary Overie, was funded by two Norman knights, who established the 'black cannons', an Augustinian order that helped the poor and needy of the area and founded a hospital dedicated to Thomas Becket. This was the forerunner of St Thomas' Hospital, now relocated to Lambeth.

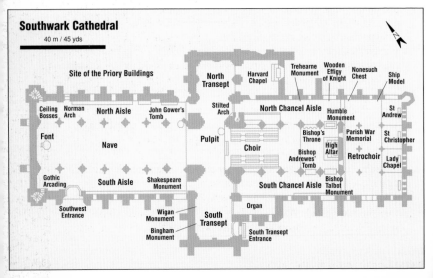

Southwark Cathedral

40 m / 45 yds

Right up until 1846 Southwark was part of the Diocese of Winchester, which stretched from the Solent to the Thames, and St Mary Overie benefited from the nearby patronage of Winchester Palace (*see page 48*). The church was thus a setting for many important occasions, especially under Cardinal Beaufort in the 15th century. In 1424 it was the scene of James I of Scotland's marriage to Joan Beaufort, the cardinal's niece.

When Henry VIII dissolved the monasteries in the 1530s, the priory church was closed and reopened as the parish church of St Saviour, Southwark. It then fell into decline, and the former cloisters were given over to light industry, including the manufacture of Delftware, and the retro-choir was rented out as a bakery and then pigsty. Revival came under James I, when a group of parishioners known as 'the Bargainers' bought the church from the king. It prospered through Elizabethan times, when it was at the centre of Bankside development, but hard times again followed in the early 19th century, by which time Southwark was growing poorer.

Restoration was favoured over demolition and, in 1905, to meet the needs of the growing population, the Southwark Diocese was created and the church attained the status of a cathedral, though it still kept its role as a parish church. To this day, anyone living within this parish, extending roughly from the Globe Theatre to Hay's Galleria, can be baptised, married or have their funeral at the cathedral.

At least four fires have broken out here, the first in 1212, after which the badly damaged Norman church was rebuilt in the Gothic style, though this new incarnation was also engulfed by flames in the 1390s. Much of the present cathedral dates from later restorations of the Gothic style, though traces of the original Norman building can still be seen in the nave. The fact that only one side of the cathedral has stained-glass windows is due to bomb damage during World War II.

Thanks to a £3.9 million grant from the National Lottery, topped up to £10 million by English Heritage and the cathedral itself, another ambitious renovation has been taking place. Works range from cleaning the stonework and relandscaping the cemetery gardens to the building of a new refectory block and a multi-media exhibition centre with connecting glass-roofed walkways.

Inside, the cathedral reflects the preoccupations of Church teaching through the ages, with many features symbolising the suffering of Christ, the despair of an unrepentant death and the agony of hell, the main themes of Church propaganda from the Middle Ages onwards. Its slightly twisted nave, rebuilt in the 15th century, is a 'weeping nave', mirroring Christ's figure on the cross.

Left and right: Southwark Cathedral

More symbols can be found on several bosses from the original wooden ceiling (out of an original complement of 150), displayed near the font, not far from the main southwest entrance. In situ, these would have been far too high for the congregation to see, yet their illiterate carvers turned them into powerful warnings and allegories. In one, the body of Judas Iscariot is being swallowed by the devil; in another a Pelican, an early symbol of Christ, is feeding its young.

The cathedral is also a rich fund of local history. A number of its memorials and chantries reflect Southwark's importance in Elizabethan and Jacobean London. The memorial to Shakespeare in the south aisle, paid for by public subscription in 1912, shows the bard reclining in front of a frieze of 16th-century Bankside, including the Globe, St Saviour's and Winchester Palace. Above it is a modern (1954) stained-glass window depicting characters from his plays. Shakespeare was a parishioner for several years; his brother Edmund, a bell-ringer at Southwark and a member of William's company of players, was buried here (the exact spot is unknown) and is commemorated by a paving stone in the floor of the choir.

Other literary figures commemorated in the cathedral include the Jacobean poets John Fletcher and Philip Massinger, who share a single grave, and the early English poet John Gower (died 1408), a friend of Geoffrey Chaucer. Gower's tomb (north aisle), a florid affair in red and green, provides a taste of the colourful paintwork that would have covered the cathedral in medieval times. Another notable medieval relic is the late 13th-century effigy of a knight (north choir aisle), one of the earliest wooden effigies of a knight in England, thought to depict a member of the De Warenne family, important benefactors of the cathedral; a dog sits at the knight's crossed feet – an indication that the knight probably died at home rather than on a crusade.

Modern memorials include one to the victims of the tragic sinking of the *Marchioness*

Above: altar screen in Southwark Cathedral
Left: the Cathedral's Shakespeare memorial

pleasure boat on the Thames in 1989 and one to the actor, director and producer Sam Wanamaker (to the right of the Shakespeare memorial), the driving force behind the rebuilding of the Globe Theatre. Interestingly, Wanamaker's is the only memorial to a Jew in a British cathedral (the 19th-century prime minister Benjamin Disraeli has a memorial in Westminster Abbey – but in the Church of England's classification that doesn't count as a cathedral).

Harvard Chapel, off the north transept, was restored to its 12th-century glory with funds from Harvard University, marking John Harvard's links with Southwark (*see page 57*). Harvard's parents lived in Southwark and their son was baptised in the cathedral in 1607; a record of the baptism is on display next to the window into the chapel from the north transept. The chapel, reserved for private prayer, contains a tabernacle by the 19th-century architect Augustus Pugin, a leader of the Gothic Revival who collaborated with Charles Barry on the Palace of Westminster.

The tower over the crossing is 15th-century. From its beautiful red-and-green coffered ceiling hangs a magnificent 16th-century brass candelabrum incorporating a bishop's mitre, a crown and the holy spirit in the shape of a dove, reflecting the relationship between Church and State. Beyond here are the choir, sanctuary and high altar, culminating in an impressive stone altar screen, commissioned by Richard Fox, Bishop of Winchester, in 1520, though the niches in the screen were not filled until the early 20th century. The retrochoir contains four chapels and the splendidly carved and decorated Nonesuch chest (1588), which held the parish records.

The grounds of the cathedral are tiny compared with those of most cathedrals, but their peaceful benches offer a welcome respite from the hubbub of nearby London Bridge. Look out for the Nancy Steps leading up the bridge: these featured in Charles Dickens's *Oliver Twist*.

Borough Market

Across Cathedral Street from Southwark Cathedral is one side of another historic institution, Borough Market. It is primarily a wholesale fruit and vegetable market, supplying restaurants and hotels in the centre of town. Trade begins in earnest at around 2am and, by the time the rest of London is waking up for work, most of the stall-holders have packed up for the day and gone for a slap-up breakfast – Borough Café on Park Street (*see page 81*) opens at 3.30am and closes after lunch – or a pint of real ale at one of the historic taverns. In addition to the normal pub hours, both the Market Porter on Stoney Street (*see page 88*) and the Globe Tavern on Bedale Street are licensed from 6am to 8.30am.

The history of 'London's Larder' can be traced back nearly 1,000 years. It started life on London Bridge – which, for centuries, was the only bridge spanning the Thames. Farmers

Right: dining out at Borough Market

and traders from all over Europe and the southern counties converged at the city's gateway to sell their produce and livestock. By the mid-18th century, the chaos and congestion on the streets around the southern end of the bridge had become so unbearable that parliament was forced to abolish the old market and find a new site. In 1756, Borough Market was

relocated to its current premises, a triangular pitch of land next to Southwark Cathedral, bounded by South-wark Street, Stoney Street and Winchester Walk. At that time, it was both a wholesale and retail market; the changeover from one to the other was announced by a bell rung at the market entrance at 10.30am.

More than 200 years on, an increasing number of food traders are selling direct to the public. There are now two retail markets a week: the Friday market (noon–6pm) attracts city workers shopping for weekend treats, while the Saturday market (9am–4pm) draws weekend shop-pers from out of town. It's not cheap by supermarket standards, but you certainly get what you pay for and, best of all, you can sample most things before you buy. Apart from organic basics such as fruit and vegetables, bread and cheese, a wide choice of more unusual food is offered, with stalls specialising in potted shrimps, smoked fish, game, mushrooms, dried fruits and nuts, wines and beers, and Spanish ingredients. If looking at all that food makes you peckish, the charcoal-grilled chorizo and rocket in a hot ciabatta roll, cooked up by the Spanish stall, is one of the best snacks around.

More information about Borough Market can be found on its website, www.londonslarder.org.uk.

Foodies should also explore the surrounding streets, where an increasing number of specialist shops are appearing in revamped old buildings. The whole area is in the throes of a regeneration programme, but something of its Dickensian character still lingers in the narrow alleyways, which have often

been used as film locations (parts of *Bridget Jones's Diary* and Guy Ritchie's *Lock, Stock and Two Smoking Barrels* were shot on Park Street).

Look out for Neal's Yard Dairy (6–8 Park Street), stacked to the ceiling with wheels of farm cheese from all over Britain; Konditor & Cook (10 Stoney Street) with its tantalising cakes, cleverly lined up en route to the cash register; De Gustibus (6 Southwark Street), the artisan bakers, twice voted 'Best Baker of the Year'; and winewinewine.co.uk (2 Bedale St), specialising in food and wine from Southwest France. The trendy restaurant fish! – you can tell it's trendy because it dispenses with capital letters – at 19 Cathedral Street *(see page 81)* also has its own (expensive) fishmonger.

Borough High Street

The west side of Borough Market faces onto **Borough High Street**, once the main road into London from the south. It intersects at this point with Southwark Street and it's worth strolling a few yards to your right down Southwark Street to see the splendid **Hop Exchange**.

Carvings above the main entrance show hop gatherers at work and, although the building now houses private offices and is not open to the public, you can glance through the main doors to see the exchange's 75-ft (23-metre) high great hall with three tiers of wrought-iron galleries looking down on the former trading floor. This part of Southwark was the centre of England's hop trade and sacks of hops brought in from Kent, Worcester and Hereford were stored in warehouses in the area before being sold to brewers. The glass roof of the Exchange allowed buyers to view the hops by natural light.

If the fruit of the vine is more to your taste than beer, note that wine importers Balls Brothers have a good wine bar in the Hop Exchange's basement *(see page 88)*. Otherwise, make your way back the junction of Southwark Street and Borough High Street and cross the street. You'll see more evidence of the hop trade in a panel carved on the front of Number 67.

Before viewing the George Inn, the most celebrated attraction on the High Street, you might wish to walk to your left (towards London Bridge) and turn right at St Thomas Street to visit the **Old Operating Theatre & Herb Garret** at Number 9A (daily 10.30am–5pm, tel: 8806 4325, recorded information; 7995 4791, museum). These are the only parts of St Thomas' Hospital to survive on its original site near London Bridge station after the hospital moved to its new location in Lambeth in 1871 (today the area is dominated by Guy's Hospital). Owing to pressure of space in a rapidly expanding part of London, the operating theatre was located in the attic of the church next to the herb garret.

As the only surviving 19th-century operating theatre in the country, it offers a gruesome but fascinating insight into both the social history of Southwark and the sometimes fearsome medical techniques of the day. The most commonly performed operations here were amputations following

Left: produce for sale in Borough Market
Right: 19th-century business sign in Borough High Street

breakages or wounds. Road accidents were a frequent cause of injury, often becoming infected as a result of insanitary living conditions and the filth and manure covering the busy streets. The female patients were brought in from the wards, sometimes blindfolded to relieve them of the ignominy of being exposed inelegantly before an audience of male medical students packed into the theatre 'like herrings in a barrel, but not so quiet'. As all operations were done without anaesthetic, the women had to be physically restrained. Only poor women would be operated on here (the wealthy would be treated at home, usually on their kitchen table). Although the surgeons were skilful, they were unaware of how infection was spread, and there was a 30 percent mortality rate within three days of an operation.

The operating theatre was in use at the same time as the church below, and a cavity between the operating theatre floor and the church ceiling was filled with sawdust to prevent blood dripping onto the worshippers.

The adjacent Herb Garret is more soothing. Here there are displays of the herbs and equipment used in the preparation of medicines in the 19th century. The apothecary, one of the most important people in the hospital, would use herbs from the hospital's herb garden or buy them in from outside. This little museum is suitable for children – guided tours can be arranged for all ages. It is equally interesting for adults, and the two curators are very willing to share their considerable knowledge with visitors. Note that entry to the museum is via a narrow spiral staircase – there's no disabled access and it can be tricky if your legs are weak.

Above: the Old Operating Theatre

The George Inn

If you feel you need a stiff drink after visiting the operating theatre, make your way back to Borough High Street where, at Number 77, an archway leads into the courtyard of the George Inn, built in 1676 and the only galleried coaching inn left in London. Because early versions of London Bridge were too narrow to carry coaches into the city, inns to accommodate them and their passengers sprang up all along the street, causing Thomas Dekker to describe it in the 17th century as 'a continued ale house with not a shop to be seen between'. The George originally surrounded three sides of the courtyard, but the central and northern wings were demolished in 1899 to make way for railway construction and the replacement buildings are none too sympathetic. To prevent further vandalism, the National Trust took over the pub in 1937 and leases it to the Whitbread brewery. The interior has some interesting old prints and photographs, but gets very crowded at lunchtimes.

Memories of Harvard and Dickens

The only trace of the George's former companions remains in the names of alleyways leading off Borough High Street: King's Head Yard, White Hart Yard, Mermaid Court. One long-gone pub, the Queen's Head, was owned by the mother of John Harvard, who was christened in what is now Southwark Cathedral *(see page 53)* and grew up in the area. After marrying in 1637, he sold the pub bequeathed to him by his mother and emigrated to Massachusetts,

becoming a pastor. But he died of tuberculosis within a year and left half his £1,600 estate to a fledgling school, renamed Harvard College in his honour. A plaque on Number 103 marks the site of the inn.

Down Union Street, on the right, at Number 171, is the dynamic **Jerwood Space** (admission free), a converted Victorian school consisting of three galleries, an outside sculpture area, café and rehearsal rooms for young theatre and dance companies. Just opposite it is the atmospheric Charles Dickens pub *(see page 87)*.

Dickens refers in his novels to several of Borough High Street's inns, and much of *Little Dorrit*, published in monthly parts in 1856 and 1857, is set in the area. The **Church of St George the Martyr**, a quarter of a mile along Borough High Street on the left, is sometimes known as 'Little Dorrit's Church' because she was baptised and married there and slept in the church one night when she was locked out of Marshalsea Prison where she then lived – and where, in real life, Dickens's father had been jailed for debt. A church has existed on this site since at least 1122 and the present building dates from 1734–36, although the bells and organ from the older church were preserved. The present font is a copy of a much older one. In 1897 an ornate plaster ceiling was added, showing cherubs celebrating the Glory of God; the cherubs were mortally injured by World

Above: the courtyard of the George Inn

War II bombing and today's ceiling is a replica. The stained-glass east window, added in 1951–52, incorporates the figure of Little Dorrit. One face of the church's clock is unlit at night, preserving a tradition dating to 1868 when gas lighting was installed but, to save money, was applied to only three of the four faces. There are recitals at 1pm on Thursdays (free but donations welcome), when you are invited to bring a packed lunch.

The **Marshalsea Prison** was closed in 1842; the only remnant is a wall by the Local Studies Library on Borough high Street, before you reach the church.

Those with a tendency to follow fire engines should turn right at the next main junction and proceed down Marshalsea Road, turning right at the end into Southwark Bridge Road. A hundred metres along, on the right at Number 94A, is the **London Fire Brigade Museum**, housed in the residence of a 19th-century brigade superintendant (admission only by pre-booked guided tours at 10.30am, 12.30pm and 2.30pm Mon–Fri; fee; tel: 7587 2894). Several vintage fire engines are on display in a hall opposite the reception area and the main house has a wide collection of historical items ranging from helmets and breathing apparatus to paintings of the blitz. Fire fighting *(see pages 12–13)* was important in a city whose rapid growth outstripped the ability of safety regulators. One early brigade chief, James Braidwood, died in the Tooley Street fire of 1861.

The Cuming Museum

If your flames of curiosity about Southwark's history are still burning, you may wish to visit the small **Cuming Museum** (155–157 Walworth Road, Tues–Sat 10am–5pm; tel: 7701 1342; admission free), which makes a big effort to give local children a taste for the past. The gift of some fossils and an old coin on his fifth birthday in 1782 inspired Richard Cuming to become a collector and the undisciplined result has been called 'the British Museum in miniature'. One speciality is London superstitions, and exhibits range from charms to ward off rheumatism and diarrhoea to tusks offering protection against the evil eye.

The museum is a dreary 15-minute walk from St George the Martyr: carry on down Borough High Street into Newington Causeway, which runs into the heavily trafficked Elephant and Castle roundabout, take the second turning to the left (Newington Butts) and turn left at the next roundabout into Walworth Road – the museum will be on your left.

If, after seeing the Cuming, you wish to proceed to the Imperial War Museum *(Itinerary 4, page 71)*, return to the Elephant and Castle roundabout and take the first left into St George's Road. The museum is five minutes' walk away, at the junction with Lambeth Road.

Above: an early motorised fire engine
Right: James Braidwood, the fire chief who died in 1861
Facing page: an alley off Borough High Street

Pool of London

3. LONDON BRIDGE TO TOWER BRIDGE

London Bridge

The present three-span **London Bridge**, dating from 1967–72, is the latest of many on this site; until 1750, when Westminster Bridge was opened, this was the only Thames crossing in the London area. The first bridge, probably made of wood, was built by the Romans around AD50. Several successors were destroyed by fire or gale. A Viking king, Olaf, tore down one, giving birth to a Saga, 'London bridge is broken down', which later became the nursery rhyme 'London Bridge is falling down'. The first stone bridge appeared in 1176 and was later lined with houses, shops and a chapel dedicated to St Thomas Becket. A fire on the 19-arch bridge in the early 13th century was said to have killed 3,000 inhabitants, firefighters and sightseers – many were trapped in the middle when both sides of the bridge caught fire. It became a custom to display the heads of executed traitors and heretics on spikes above the bridge; in 1598 a German visitor counted 30 heads.

In 1823–31, a new bridge of five stone arches was built. When it was replaced in 1972 by the present pre-stressed concrete structure, it was dismantled and re-erected at Lake Havasu in Arizona. It was a popular joke that the American buyer thought he was acquiring the next bridge downstream, the spectacular Tower Bridge.

To the east of the bridge is **London Bridge Station**, which is very much a rush-hour station shuttling commuters from the southeast suburbs and beyond. The first steam trains arrived here in 1836 and, as more railway companies began using it, an imposing Italianate building was constructed. Trains from Greenwich were carried on 878 Doric arches, resembling a Roman viaduct. The station was badly bombed during World War II. Today it is linked to the London Underground system (Jubilee Line and one branch of the Northern Line).

London Dungeon

Tucked beneath the northern side of London Bridge Station on Tooley Street, the **London Dungeon** (daily Oct–Mar 10am–5.30pm/last admission 4.30pm, Apr–Sep 10am–6.30pm/last admission 5.30pm, later in July and August; admission charge; tel: 09001 600066) takes you on a scary journey through the catacombs of old London town. The tour begins with an obligatory photo opportunity – head in the stocks, a blackened chopper at your neck. The visitor is plunged into darkness, and it takes a while to adjust

Left: Tower Bridge
Right: pausing by the river

to the gloom. The atmosphere is pretty spooky as cell after cell reveals an assortment of reprobates in ever more torturous positions. Bloodcurdling screams issue from mechanical waxwork figures: an executioner garottes some pathetic soul, while another vomits blood into an overflowing barrel.

The ecclesiastical section contains the figure of a kneeling Anne Boleyn muttering prayers and blinking. Because her features have been projected

onto her, this is the most realistic and affecting piece in the exhibition. There are cases displaying a variety of devices used in bygone days; one such item is the chastity belt forced upon women when their God-fearing husbands rode off to the Crusades. The card informs us that many a man became expert at picking the locks of these gruesome implements, hence the plethora of Smiths (locksmiths, not blacksmiths) in Britain today.

After the inanimate section comes a trawl through Jack the Ripper's East End of London, with actors taking the visitor through clues to his identity. This is slightly tedious (you feel a little as if you are on a school trip as you are herded from one scenario to another).

The Judgement Day boat trip, where visitors journey through Traitors' Gate aboard barges, is accompanied by cries and screams – both as part of the exhibition and from the more nervous of the tourists. Next you are ushered into the London of the Black Plague, followed by the Great Fire of 1666 (predicted by a talking head of the prophet Nostradamus), with the atmosphere recreated by dry ice and an increasingly stuffy room. Terrified shrieks can be heard in the distance while you are exhorted to run for your life through a maze of hot corridors, arriving at a rotating tunnel with a kaleidoscopic array of fiery colours, before being ejected into fluorescent-lit reality and the chance to purchase your photograph for a fiver. There is a souvenir shop and café-bar.

Winston Churchill's Britain at War Experience

Just beyond the London Dungeon is an attraction graphically detailing a more modern example of man's inhumanity to man. World War II hit Southwark worse than most areas of London as German bombers targeted its docks and warehouses, and this museum at 64–66 Tooley Street (daily 10am–last admission 4.30pm Oct–Mar, 5.30pm Apr–Sept; admission charge; tel: 7403 3171) tries to recreate the sounds and smells of the blitz through special effects, illustrating what life was like in an air raid shelter and showing the aftermath of a bombing raid. Wartime news is projected in an underground cinema, and there are lots of wartime posters, magazine covers, newspaper cuttings and extracts

Above: a doorman at the London Dungeon
Right: a Britain at War Experience exhibit

from Sir Winston Churchill's speeches. Clothes, radios, toys and toilet paper from the 1940s conjure up an exotically different age, and retired GIs may view a Wurlitzer jukebox and Varga pin-ups with a certain nostalgia. A wrecked drapery store cunningly uses tailors' dummies to suggest carnage without having to portray real mutilation. School parties have great fun trying on helmets and gas masks, but children might benefit most from the exhibition if, before visiting, they were given a quick briefing about the war.

On the opposite side of the road is **Hay's Galleria**, a glittering complex of restaurants *(see page 82)* and shops (including a good bookshop and an unusual store selling only products relating to Christmas). Its high vaulted roof recalling the grandeur of the old warehouses. Hay's Wharf, the Port of London's oldest wharf, pioneered cold storage for dairy goods in the 1860s.

HMS Belfast

Walk through the galleria and you will reach the Thames Path. Turn right, passing the ornate Horniman pub, and after a leisurely five-minute walk you will reach *HMS Belfast* (Mar–Oct 10am–6pm, Nov–Feb 10am–5pm, closed 24–26 Dec; admission charge; disabled access on two of the nine decks, tel: 7940 6300). Moored just upstream from Tower Bridge, this is Britain's only surviving example of the big-gun armoured warships built during the first half of the 20th century. Now part of the Imperial War Museum *(see page 71)*, it gives a fascinating insight into the work of a warship and the strains of life on board. Launched in Belfast in 1938, the vessel was in active service until 1965, and served in World War II and Korea. As a 'cruiser', or flagship, it played an important role in leading convoys.

The recommended tour (free map provided) begins on the quarterdeck, proceeds via the boatdeck to the bridge and gun turret 'A', then descends via the living quarters to the boiler and engine rooms. Gun turret 'A' is one

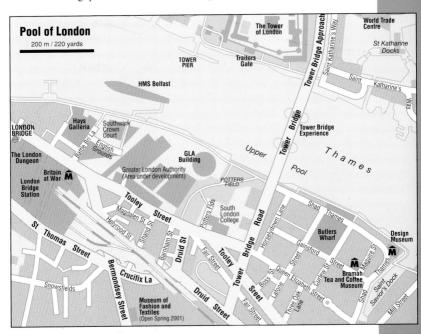

Pool of London

200 m / 220 yards

World Trade Centre
St Katharine Docks
The Tower of London
TOWER PIER
Traitors Gate
Tower Bridge Approach
Saint Katharine's Way
Saint Katharine's
HMS Belfast
LONDON BRIDGE
Hays Galleria
Southwark Crown Court
English Grounds
Battle Bri La
Tower Bridge
Tower Bridge Experience
The London Dungeon
GLA Building
Upper
Thames
Britain at War
Greater London Authority (Area under development)
POTTERS FIELD
Pool
London Bridge Station
Tooley Street
Magdalen St
Holyrood St
Shand St
Potters Flds
South London College
Shad Thames
Horselydown Lane
Shad
Butlers Wharf
Design Museum
St Thomas Street
Barnham St
Druid St
Fair Street
Tooley
Tooley Street
Tower Bridge Road
Gainsford
Street
Queen Elizabeth Street
Three Oak Lane
Boss Street
Latone
Courley St
Bramah Tea and Coffee Museum
Saint Saviors Dock
Maguire St
Mill Street
Shad
Bermondsey Street
Crucifix La
Snowsfields
Druid Street
Fair Street
Museum of Fashion and Textiles
(Open Spring 2001)

of four such turrets, each of which would have been manned by a team of 27 highly trained men able to launch eight rounds of shells a minute from each gun. The guns could be used against land and sea targets up to 23 km (14 miles) away – the ones in turret 'A' are currently trained on a service station 20km (12 miles) up the M1 motorway. It is worth venturing down into the heavily armoured shell room below the gun-turret, where a further 22 men would have sent the shells up to the gun room by mechanical hoist. A secondary battery of anti-aircraft mountings located on either side of the ship could be used against enemy planes up to 39,000 ft (11,900 metres) away, supported by the massive Bofor guns on either side of the bridge.

At the height of its career the *Belfast* accommodated 950 men. In the 1950s it was refitted, and life for the sailors improved dramatically, with the addition of showers, proper bunk beds, a laundry and a modern kitchen with the same fittings as the Royal Yacht *Britannia*. Most of what you see belongs to the 1950s revamp, but a portion has been returned to its original, commissioned state, with cramped messes slung with hammocks only 21 inches (52 cm) apart.

As the 'mother' ship in the fleet, the *Belfast* was equipped with an operating theatre, a dental surgery and hospital beds, as well as extensive food and ammunition stores, a butcher and bakery, where a team of six bakers would keep the fleet in fresh bread. All these facilities are on display, with wax dummies, sound effects and plenty of props. But what really brings the boat to life is the archive footage of the *Belfast* in action. This includes the moving story of the destruction of the German battlecruiser *Scharnhorst* in the Battle of North Cape in World War II, when only 36 out of the

1,963 Germans on board survived, and an account of the *Belfast*'s role in the Normandy Landings of 1944.

Less bloody battles may be enacted in the oval-shaped office building under construction by the river here. It is designated as the **headquarters of the Greater London Authority** – successor to the Greater London Council (which occupied County Hall until 1986) and to be presided over by the GLC's former leader, Ken Livingstone, who was elected as London's mayor in 2000. Its expanse of glass is meant to signify the new authority's transparency, but the mischievous Mr Livingstone dismissed it as 'a giant glass testicle'.

Tower Bridge Experience

Dominating the area is **Tower Bridge**, one of London's most distinctive and frequently photographed landmarks. In the 19th century, a time of great industrial expansion, there was a pressing need to improve circulation over the river without hindering the access of ships into London's docks. The result was this triumph of Victorian engineering, constructed between 1886 and 1894, a steel frame held together with 3 million rivets, clad with decorative stonework in High Gothic style. It was opened amid great celebration by the Prince and Princess of Wales on 30 June 1894. The current red, white and blue paintwork dates from the Queen's Silver Jubilee in 1977.

The entrance to the **Tower Bridge Experience** (10am–6.30pm Apr–Oct, 9.30am–6pm Nov–Mar; admission charge; tel: 7378 1928) is near the northern bank of the Thames. With the aid of audio-visual and interactive displays, the semi-guided tour takes visitors through the history of the bridge, from the controversy that raged over the need to construct it at all, right through to its electrification in 1977. The tour gives you the chance to see most of the inside of the bridge: down in the basement, inside the two turrets and along

the raised walkways, from where you have a spectacular view of London on a clear day. The highlight on the walkways is a great collection of old photographs showing the progress of the building work on the bridge – a tourist attraction in its own right at the time.

The photographs of the views from the bridge from the 1880s onwards illustrate clearly the massive changes that have taken place in the city in the past 100 years. The docks to the east, once the 'warehouse of the world', have all but disappeared, and just to the west of the bridge there was a small 'beach' on the banks on the Thames used by Londoners for a day out.

For those interested in engineering, there is plenty of detail and hands-on displays on how the bascules operate, and the original hydraulic equipment is preserved in immaculate condition. For details of when the bridge is scheduled to be raised, tel: 7378 7700.

Top left: how the new Greater London Authority building will look
Left: *HMS Belfast*. **Above:** Tower Bridge

Butlers Wharf

To the east of Tower Bridge is a lovingly restored riverside thoroughfare, Shad Thames, whose narrow streets and small walkways have long been a favourite location for many period films and dramas including *Oliver!* (1967) and *The Elephant Man* (1980). Shad Thames is a corruption of St John at Thames, which refers to the Knights Templar, who once controlled the area. Overhead walkways – initially designed to transport goods among what

were once warehouses and are now converted flats – provide excellent glimpses of the area's rich heritage. On the left as you make your way past Shad Thames's many shops is an archway that opens onto Butlers Wharf.

Situated between two historic conservation acres, Tower Bridge and St Saviour's Dock, **Butlers Wharf** was originally completed in 1873. Once the largest warehouse complex on the River Thames and a major dock for tea, coffee, and spices, its Victorian buildings became derelict after it closed in 1972. In 1985 a development team chaired by the retailer and restaurateur Sir Terence Conran began transforming the area's unlisted and Grade II listed buildings into a shopping, dining and residential area at a cost of £100 million. *(For restaurants, see pages 82–3).*

Conservation issues surrounding the development of Butlers warehouses, 17 of which are listed buildings, meant lengthy and complicated compromises with English Heritage and the Royal Fine Arts Commission. To preserve the rich visual history and architectural integrity of Butlers Wharf, great efforts were made to refurbish existing buildings that were sound and to

Top: old and new buildings at Shad Thames
Above: watching the boats go by at Butlers Wharf

replace only those structures that were in poor shape. But a subsequent recession in the property market resulted in several new projects of questionable design quality which some critics view as disappointing blemishes on the initial vision for restoring the Butlers Wharf area.

A walk along Butlers Wharf allows you to view the ebb and flow of the Thames as well as its many birds – watch out for herons – boats, delicate scents, and changing colours. The enthusiasm of visitors, especially on sunny days, is infectious, while on duller days London's famously grey skies and rain lend their own mysterious charm to the picturesque streets of this area.

The Design Museum

Many old warehouses in the Butlers Wharf area have been converted into luxurious apartments, occupied by wealthy and design-conscious people. It's appropriate, therefore, that the gleaming white **Design Museum** (Mon–Fri 11.30am–6pm, Sat–Sun 10.30am–6pm; admission charge; tel: 7378-6055) is located at the eastern end of Shad Thames.

Originally a 1950s warehouse, the Design Museum was converted in the modern style by the architects Conran Roche and first opened its doors in 1989. The museum's founder, Sir Terence Conran, whose successful Habitat and Conran home-furnishing shops and series of fashionable restaurants can be found throughout London, originally set up the Boilerhouse design project in the Victoria and Albert Museum; when the V&A declined to make it permanent, Conran turned his attention to Butlers Wharf. Although he initially intended to restore the old warehouse, in the end it proved less expensive to strip much of the existing structure down to its steel skeleton and rebuild it.

The Design Museum, whose elegant, layered front commands stunning views of the River Thames and Tower Bridge, is Europe's first museum dedicated to the exploration and study of modern design for mass production. How an object looks, who it will be used by, what it is made of, its feel, cost and weight, are all elements of design that are explored through the museum's permanent and temporary exhibits.

Make your way up the wide, white marble stairs past the glass brick walls to the Temporary and Exhibition Galleries on the first floor. This simple, white space acts as a blank canvas for temporary exhibits of intriguing subjects such as Bauhaus – one of the 20th century's most influential design schools – and alternative urban housing.

The oak floors of the Design Museum's Collection and Review Galleries, located on the second floor, are bathed in natural light, with high ceilings and vast windows accentuating the tremendous views. Here visitors can wander amid a series of thematic product displays; these chronicle the evolution of now commonplace articles such as television sets – including a 1969 white, round TV set which heralded the arrival of the 'space-age' – cameras, telephones (e.g. the 1895 Skeleton Telephone) and even plastic packaging. Samples of past, present and future design innovations show that function and aesthetics can go hand in hand.

Right: a heady experience in front of the Design Museum

Situated on the ground floor overlooking Shad Thames is the museum café, which offers reasonably priced light lunches and, if you're lucky, a seat overlooking Tower Bridge. Not to be missed is the museum shop, which offers a selection of books as well as entertaining and unusual gift ideas from analogue cuff-links to glass teapots. There is a lift for disabled visitors, and the shop, café and all exhibits are wheelchair accessible.

As a special treat, there's Terence Conran's Blue Print Café (*see page 83*). It can be entered from the front left-hand side of the museum, and has elegant but pricey European and Mediterranean cuisine, plus lovely river views.

Bramah Tea & Coffee Museum

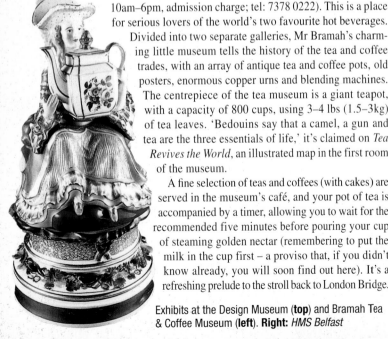

As you stroll back on Shad Thames, turn down Maguire Street to find, at Number 1, the **Bramah Tea and Coffee Museum** (daily 10am–6pm, admission charge; tel: 7378 0222). This is a place for serious lovers of the world's two favourite hot beverages. Divided into two separate galleries, Mr Bramah's charming little museum tells the history of the tea and coffee trades, with an array of antique tea and coffee pots, old posters, enormous copper urns and blending machines. The centrepiece of the tea museum is a giant teapot, with a capacity of 800 cups, using 3–4 lbs (1.5–3kg) of tea leaves. 'Bedouins say that a camel, a gun and tea are the three essentials of life,' it's claimed on *Tea Revives the World*, an illustrated map in the first room of the museum.

A fine selection of teas and coffees (with cakes) are served in the museum's café, and your pot of tea is accompanied by a timer, allowing you to wait for the recommended five minutes before pouring your cup of steaming golden nectar (remembering to put the milk in the cup first – a proviso that, if you didn't know already, you will soon find out here). It's a refreshing prelude to the stroll back to London Bridge.

Exhibits at the Design Museum (**top**) and Bramah Tea & Coffee Museum (**left**). **Right:** *HMS Belfast*

Imperial War Museum

4. FROM WATERLOO TO THE IMPERIAL WAR MUSEUM

Lambeth North is the closest Underground station to the museum. Walk down Kennington Road, which is directly across the five-way junction from the station entrance, and turn left into Lambeth Road. You will shortly see on your right the huge double guns in front of the imposing neoclassical building that houses the Imperial War Museum.

If you are starting from Waterloo Station, an interesting route to the museum will take you through one of London's oldest street markets. Follow the Waterloo Road signs to exit from the sprawling station and turn right on Waterloo Road. You will see the **Old Vic** theatre to the left of a main junction. This elegant landmark, built in 1816–18, has had a chequered history, from its early days as a temperance music hall to its more illustrious status as the first home of the National Theatre under the direction of Sir Laurence Olivier and its present incarnation as a repertory theatre. Its recent economic problems have partly been the result of its 1,067-seat capacity: it's a bit big for intimate productions but too small for large-scale shows. However, the dance company Adventures in Motion is due to become company-in-residence in 2002. (Further down The Cut, on the left, is the **Young Vic**, an intimate open-space theatre with a good reputation for experimental work.)

Turn right at the main junction into Baylis Road (named after Lilian Baylis, who ran the Old Vic with great success in the first decades of the 20th century) and bear right into **Lower Marsh**. In the 19th century this accommodated London's longest street market, stretching for a mile. Today only a few dozen stalls are left, selling mainly cheap clothes, household goods and compact discs. The street has some interesting small shops, such as antiques emporia selling retro clothes and designer items from the 1930s and '40s and a bookshop specialising in transport titles.

At the far end of Lower Marsh, turn left onto Westminster Bridge Road and, when you reach Lambeth North Tube station, follow the directions above (and see map on page 74) to reach the **Imperial War Museum** (daily 10am–6pm, with free admission after 4.30pm and always free for under-16s; tel: 7416 5439). The building opened in 1815 to house the Bethlem Royal Hospital for the insane, popularly known as Bedlam and an inspired choice for a museum chronicling the horrors of modern warfare. After the hospital moved out of London in the 1930s, the central block of the building, whose wings had been demolished, was turned over to the Great War collection of the Imperial War Museum, previously housed in South Kensington. After World War II – during which,

Left and right: interior and exterior of the Imperial War Museum

ironically, the museum was damaged in air raids – it also began to gather material from this and later conflicts, and three smaller sites, including the warship *HMS Belfast (see page 63)*, were acquired to accommodate it.

There's so much to see that this is an ideal outing for a rainy afternoon: you need two to three hours to explore the main part of the museum, and at least another hour to see the Holocaust Exhibition. Over the past 10 years, the Imperial War Museum has expanded its remit from the purely military to include a rolling programme of exhibitions covering many aspects of modern history, often only loosely connected with conflict – from code breaking and refugees to fashion and sport. Many of these exhibits are aimed at the young – see the leaflets *What's On* and *What's On for Children* for details. The entrance fee covers everything including the cinema, which shows newsreels and wartime films.

As you enter the main hall, your direction will depend on where your interest lies. The stairs at the back of the Large Exhibits Gallery lead down to exhibitions on the two world wars. Here physical artefacts, art, photography, film and sound recordings weave an atmosphere as close as possible to the mood of the time, while interactive screens give access to further information.

All this film and sound can be quite an assault on the senses. It is better to settle on a particular section and absorb the small details. Looking at a letter informing a father of his son's death brings it all down to the human level. Official material such as Field-Marshal Bernard Montgomery's papers, Hitler's will and the overoptimistic 'piece of paper' prime minister Neville Chamberlain waved on his return from meeting Hitler in Munich in 1938 are interspersed with the letters, diaries, sketches and interviews of ordinary soldiers, civilians, prisoners of war, conscientious objectors and refugees. Also on show are manuscripts of war literature, such as Siegfried Sassoon's *Memoirs of an Infantry Officer*, and a room full of Victoria and George Crosses awarded for heroic deeds.

The Blitz and Trench 'experiences' may appeal more to children than adults. There is no

Imperial War Museum

This floor plan will help you find your way around the Museum. You will find further information on your ticket and there are direction signs on all floors to temporary as well as permanent exhibitions.

4   Temporary exhibition

3   Holocaust exhibition

2   Art galleries
      John Singer Sargent room

1   Secret War
      Victoria Cross and
         George Cross
      Survival at Sea:
         Merchant Navy

G   Large exhibits
      Temporary exhibitions
      Holocaust exhibition
         ticket desk
      Information
      Shop and café   **Main entrance**

LG   Historical displays
      Trench Experience
      Blitz Experience   **West entrance**

queue at the Trench, but you can see why: it's inexplicably dark and not especially realistic, though the sense of smell is quite effective: an unpleasant musty odour gives way to the sharpness of disinfectant as you pass the hospital tent. You may have to queue for the Blitz Experience, which works better than the Trench. The darkness in which you wait for air raids is atmospheric and recorded announcements help to create tension. You even get a healthy dose of dust from collapsed buildings.

Upstairs is an extension of the Large Exhibits Gallery. On the right as you come up the stairs is an aeroplane fuselage that you can walk through. The Secret War exhibit on counter-intelligence is also on this floor. Juxtaposed with the glamour of fictional spies is the harsh reality of espionage. Of six female World War II spies in one display, only one survived the war. There's a cyanide capsule, to be taken if captured – this one was handed in by an agent who luckily didn't have to use it.

The second floor holds one of Britain's leading collections of 20th-century art – the World War I gallery is to the right; World War II to the left. Many of the works were officially commissioned for propaganda purposes, including the famous painting *Gassed* in the John Singer Sargent room. The London Blitz drawings by Henry Moore are very fine.

The Holocaust Exhibition

Occupying the next two floors is the **Holocaust Exhibition**, the largest display of its kind in the world outside Israel and the United States. It will take you a good hour to look around and to listen to the large amount of video and film available. Be warned: this is an intense and harrowing exhibition and it is not advisable to bring children (there is a lower age limit of 13, but it's not strictly enforced). It is built around the testimonies of a selection of survivors who tell of their experiences chronologically from

Above: items from the Holocaust Exhibition

the origins of anti-Semitism through to its horrific conclusion. Film footage accompanies the stories, as does rare and important historical material, some of it lent by former concentration camps in eastern Europe. Larger items include a section of a deportation railcar, the entrance to a gas chamber, a dissection table, shoes collected from victims of the gas chambers and a large model of part of Auschwitz.

Especially poignant are personal belongings such as the letters of an eight-year-old Austrian boy, Georgy Halpern, who hid in an orphanage until he was betrayed and deported to Auschwitz. After he was gassed, his mother's last letter to him, also on display, was returned to her marked 'No longer at this address'. Equally chilling are the logbooks of concentration camp killings, meticulously kept by Nazi bureaucrats, and the original plans for the gas chambers. The Holocaust Exhibition marks a change of emphasis for the museum, from documenting the mechanics of warfare to exploring the effects on the victims, but even so punches had to be pulled. 'We had to strike a balance between accessibility and sheer horror in order to ensure that the exhibition is endurable,' said its director, Suzanne Bardgett.

The Imperial War Museum caters for scholars as well as casual visitors. The dome above the entrance hall houses a large reference library which is open to the public; however, because the reading room is small, it must be booked two weeks in advance. The museum doesn't hold personal service records – these are held by the Public Record Office – but if you want to find out about a family member involved in one of the wars, you're free to do independent research and the library staff will point you in the right direction.

The museum holds the world's largest sound archive (32,000 hours) and the oldest film archive (120 million feet of film from as early as 1917), as well as more than 6 million photographs, 30,000 international war posters and substantial collections of maps. Many items are displayed in the exhibits, but if you're looking for something in particular, you can have free access to the archives by appointment. Programme makers seeking footage for television documentaries on the world wars provide a useful source of revenue.

In order to digest what you've seen in the museum, you might wish to relax in the delicately symmetrical Peace Garden, opened by the Dalai Lama in 1999. It's to the right of the manicured flowerbeds as you exit the museum.

Right: the Imperial War Museum's Peace Garden

Leisure Activities

EATING OUT

South Bank

County Hall

There's **McDonald's**, which looks a tad out of place in this stately building, plus three dining places serving Chinese food, *faux* French and Italian. The **County Hall Restaurant** (tel: 7902 8000, booking advised) at least attempts a British ambience, with wood panelling and hotel-like carpets; the French-style food is decent but lacks sparkle. The restaurant comes into its own as a venue for an early-bird power breakfast (6.30–11am), where foreign clients will be knocked out by the setting, or for a morning weekend treat (7–11 am). Eight tureens polished to a high gloss dispense excellent scrambled eggs, good black pudding and mediocre waffles; service is cordial. Afternoon tea is served in the old Greater London Council library, which provides enough olde-worlde ambiance to satisfy even the most jaded of tourists, but be sure to book. **The Four Regions** (tel: 7928 0988, booking advised) is an up-market Chinese where take-away would be a crime; the view, especially in summer when tables are moved to the outdoor terrace and Big Ben takes the place of a watch, almost makes up for the standard dining fare. **Shino's Bar & Grill**, (no tel), just down from the London Eye, dispenses pasta and calamari and is a good place to pass the time away from the crowds.

Royal Festival Hall

The concert hall has four places to eat: one buffet-style cafeteria on the side of the main foyer; one café near the riverside walkway; one coffee bar with take-away snacks and one 'destination restaurant'. One of the first top-class restaurants to capitalise on its spectacular setting was Level 3's **The People's Palace** (tel: 7928 9999, booking advised).

The decor's a bit earnest, but the room's spacious proportions are reminiscent of an old-style brasserie where diners can choose to look at each other or at the river. The Palace gets temporarily mobbed after a concert – it's a good idea to book for around 8.30pm when everyone else will be listening to Verdi next door. Food is 'modern global' which means dishes like soya-braised duck with fennel and *pak choi*; the fixed-priced menus are particularly good value. *Top tip:* **Café 51**, the Festival Hall's cafeteria, is open all day. Although the food is only so-so, it's useful to know about during the 'dead zone' of 3–6pm, when other restaurants close.

Royal National Theatre

The National has five places to eat and drink (six if you include the **Film Café** at the National Film Theatre next door). The ground-floor **Lyttelton Buffet** is good for a quick pre-show meal. The **Mezzanine Restaurant** (tel: 7452 3600, booking advised) has a chequered history but reasonable food and is a predictably good place for people-watching and actor-spotting. The **Long Bar** and the **Espresso Bar** are mainly for drinks but also serve snacks. The National's best-kept secret (because it's so hard to find) is the **Terrace Café** (tel: 7452 3555), a reasonably priced brasserie with outdoor dining on sunny days, tasty, non-fussy food, and a relaxed atmosphere rare in restaurants with fine river views. *Top tip:* take the *glass* lift (not the regular lift) opposite the Long Bar to the second floor.

Left: pasta at Butlers Wharf
Right: lunching al fresco

Gabriel's Wharf

Gabriel's Wharf is flanked by two river-side restaurants, both with some outdoor tables. The more popular is the often frenetic **Gourmet Pizza Company** (tel: 7928 3188), where the inventive use of toppings brings in carnivores and vegetarians alike. The portions are filling, the salads big and fresh, and the prices reasonable. Facing it is **Riviera** (tel: 7401 7314), with an upstairs room where the decibel level matches the smooth view. It has standard Mediterranean fare and staff who can seem perplexed. **Studio Six**, further inland in Gabriel's Wharf, is a bar which has food, while the **House of Crepes** and **Sarni's** cater mainly to the daytime snack crowd.

Oxo Tower Restaurant

When this eighth-floor rooftop restaurant, brasserie and bar opened at Barge House Street in 1996, the great, the good and the vainglorious queued for tables in droves, as often as not clad in glad rags from the Oxo's sleek parent company, Knightsbridge department store Harvey Nichols. Things have calmed down, but the Oxo is still a 'destination restaurant', and it's a good idea to book (tel: 7803 3888).

The dinner menu features 'classics with a twist' (poached Scottish wild salmon served in a vegetable nage) and tends to be pricey (£21 for the salmon); better value is lunch at the brasserie where the same money will get you two courses, a glass of wine and a coffee. Other than linen tablecloths and the menu, there's little to distinguish between the restaurant and the brasserie; the interior is designed in lofty airport-hanger style, the better to be seen and to see the fantastic view out over the river.

In winter, all this chrome and glass tends to make the tables by the window a bit draughty as the wind whips in from the river, but in summer, dining on the terrace outside is one of the best South Bank experiences. The terrace shares space with the hard-to-find public viewing gallery (*see page 34*), and the restaurant management does not look approvingly on these non-diners. Anyone who wants a taste of Oxo without the attitude should slip in and have a drink in the

Top: a restaurant right beside the river
Left: eating at the Oxo Tower

bar (south-facing view, but still interesting), then exercise their right to enjoy the river with the other interlopers into glossyland.

On the ground floor, by the riverside, is **EAT**, a cute snack bar with some of the tastiest fast-food around. All ingredients are fresh, and the bread is baked daily in EAT's own kitchens. You can order a sandwich and espresso to go and picnic by the Tate, or sit outside in the sunshine at a table in the courtyard around the back.

Beyond the riverside

RSJ (tel: 7928 4554; booking advised) stands for Rolled Steel Joist, not an obvious name for a cool and rather sophisticated two-storey French-style restaurant tucked away at 13A Coin Street. Prettily arranged with paintings on the walls and a clean and crisp decor, RSJ's smooth service and wonderful wine list (mainly of undiscovered treasures from the Loire region; RSJ has an import business) make this a perfect spot for either lunch or dinner. A typical main course is noisettes of rabbit stuffed with prunes and apples; dessert might be prune and Armagnac tart. Prices are reasonable and the good-value three-course set menu changes often.

The **RSJ Café** (corner of Cornwall and Stamford streets) is the place to go for designer sandwiches.

Around The Cut

Take the Waterloo Road exit from Waterloo Station and turn right on Waterloo Road to find the **Fire Station** (tel: 7620 2226). To reach a table in the back of the noisy, disused fire station, diners have to push their way through hordes of happy drinkers. From a visible kitchen, chefs prepare ambitious specials such as ostrich steak with sweet potato hash, plus inventive starters and puds. The daily menu is chalked up twice daily on a huge blackboard. Reasonably priced and open on Sunday evenings (a rarity), the Fire Station won the *Good Pub Guide*'s 'Dining Pub of the Year' award.

Across the street from the Fire Station is **Thai Silk** (tel: 7620 2226) and down tiny Sandell Street under the railway arches is the **Auberge** bistro (tel: 7633 0610). Lower Marsh Market, the first street to the right

of the Fire Station, contains several restaurants, the best of which are the old-style Italian **Restaurant La Barca** (tel: 7928 3336) and the newer **Cubana Café** (tel: 7928 8778).

The Cut, with the Old Vic Theatre at one end and Southwark Underground station at the other, has acquired a notable concentration of restaurants. Ace local bakers **Konditor & Cook** (tel: 7620 2700) supply the heavenly cakes and savoury snacks in the café of the Young Vic Theatre, while **R. Cooke** (tel: 7928 5931) is one of the last of London's eel, pie 'n' mash shops. The liquor (non-alcoholic gravy) poured over the pie is a startling shade of green similar to Konditor's interior, but eating eels is a Cockney experience unique to London. Further down, towards Southwark Underground station, is an informal, converted pub called **Bar Citrus** (no tel), where the specialities include 'beef and bombardier pie' (Scotch beef slow-cooked in ale).

On the opposite side of The Cut are two old standbys, the **South Bank Tandoori** (tel: 7928 6127) and **Meson don Felipe** (tel: 7928 3237) – the latter serving much praised *tapas* and many sherries and Spanish wines. The **Honest Goose** (tel: 7261 1612) is a casual establishment with daily specials and low prices. It's a sister to the Honest Cabbage in Bermondsey, which non-trendy residents in the Tower Bridge area swear by. Further along is the fish restaurant **Livebait** (tel: 7620 2226; booking advised), the first restaurant in The Cut to lure media people. Its 'classic platter' consists of succulent Dorset crab

Right: Cuban cocktails by Lower Marsh's street market

ilar to the gallery's second-level café but without the latter's fetching electric-halo lights. The dinner menu has seared calves' liver and the like, but the ambience suits lunch better. Both places serve food throughout Tate Modern's opening hours (10am–6pm Sun–Thurs; 10am–10pm Fri, Sat). *Top tip:* culture vultures in need of a cigarette should head for the riverside terrace by the fourth-level espresso bar; look for the neon exhibit that reads '*Run from Fear/Fun from Rear*'.

Bankside's class act is **Shakespeare's Globe Restaurant** (tel: 7928 9444, booking advised), with its sparkling crystal, linen table-cloths and views over St Paul's Cathedral through vaguely Elizabethan-looking mullioned windows. Tables are far enough apart for diners to indulge in heated debates of a theatrical nature without disturbing their neighbours, who tend to be a fairly sophisticated bunch, often including a well-known 'luvvie' or two. An early plan to service 'authentic Elizabethan fare' mercifully failed; instead dishes favour the modern British style of cooking, with meats like leg of lamb or rib-eye steak, and lighter dishes like parcels of pastry stuffed with globe artichokes (is this a pun?). The café one floor below serves simpler dishes but is equally pleasing. In the afternoon, the café (open until 6pm) serves a reasonably-priced cream tea.

Also satisfying Bankside's cultural appetites are two eating places – one in an art gallery, one in a theatre – each sharing its name with its address. **Café One Seven One** is located in the Jerwood Space (171 Union Street, tel: 7654 0100) serves simple home-cooking, which is vegetarian-friendly – try the cous-cous burger. Prices are low and the soups are great; closed in the evening. **Sixty-two** (62 Southwark Bridge Road, tel: 7633 0831) is the restaurant space attached to – but not part of – the Southwark Playhouse. Prices are comparable to the mid-level river-bank restaurants, but Sixty-two's off-the-beaten-track location makes for a more intimate occasion. Further away, **Delfina** (50 Bermondsey Street, tel: 7357 0244) continues the trend of reliable cooking in good-looking studio spaces, with a calm, cool decor and tables so far apart you could rollerblade right through them. Stop by for lunch when you're near London Bridge.

and/or Nova Scotia lobster, while the catches of the day are pencilled in on the menus outside. Some feel its standards aren't quite what they were, but they're still pretty good.

Towards Blackfrairs Road, **Tas** (7928 1444) offers clean, healthy, often vegetarian food at reasonable prices served in a stylish atmosphere. It's billed as a Turkish restaurant, but a dish like spinach and orange salad seems more a tasty, trendy invention than a traditional Turkish delight. The menu is long and confusing (the staff short-handed and confused), but strange dishes like *Icli kofte* and *patlican dolmasi* are successful, as are the more recognisable cous cous and kabobs. The set menu is good for sampling lots of different dishes. *Top tip:* unless you've just got back from a holiday in Istanbul, avoid the Turkish wine.

Bankside

Tate Modern Café (tel: 7401 5020, booking advised for dinner) in located in the penthouse of the former power station. Escalators end abruptly two floors below the seventh-level restaurant, right by the *Nude/Action/Body* exhibit. Trying to find the stairs to continue upwards can involve an inadvertent trip through Turner-Prize winner Steve McQueen's video installation *Bear*, so by the time diners reach the 170-seater eatery with its long, narrow layout and widespread river views, they'll have worked up an appetite. Lunch is corn-fed chicken, shepherd's pie, sandwiches or pasta, a menu sim-

Above: fresh fish in The Cut
Right: more of the same at fish! near Southwark Cathedral

eating out

The Borough

The Borough, astonishingly packed with pubs and sandwich bars, has in recent years acquired some decent restaurants. **Simply Nico** (tel: 7407 4536), part of the London Bridge Hotel close to the railway station, has a clean, corporate feel that appeals to 'the suits' in the area with healthy expense accounts. The main courses – such as seared scallops and artichoke galettes – are equally modern.

Even more modern is **fish!** (tel: 7234 3333, booking advised), a greenhouse-like structure between Southwark Cathedral and Borough Market. The menu policy favours the kitchen rather than the customer (diners tick their order on a pre-printed list of the day's catches, cutting down the need for staff) and service can be careless, though the fish itself is succulent and fresh. It's not a place for quiet conversation: noise bounces off the stylish glass walls at ever increasing levels. *Top tip:* a seat at the bar will expose you to a deafening combination of noise from the kitchen and the dining tables.

Vinopolis, London's museum of wine around the corner from fish!, is building into its huge vaults a series of eating places and wine-drinking spaces. The first to open was **Cantina Vinopolis** (tel: 7940 8333), with wooden tables huddled refectory-like under soaring 'cathedral' arches, with an open-view kitchen at the far end. Despite a bustling atmosphere, service is efficient and the staff unflustered. Food is pleasant, with starters like pumpkin and parmesan soup with lime crème fraîche; mains like seared blue fin tuna on a warm potato confit, tomato and chorizo salad, finishing off with Cantina Vinopolis trifle. The wine list is long, with more than 200 different types available by the glass. Around the corner on Stoney Street is the **Wine Wharf**. Over 100 different wines can be ordered by the glass here, along with a range of tasty tapas which change daily and are sold at the affordable price of four for £4.50. *Top tip:* take your treats to the top floor of the Wine Wharf, where leather sofas, daily newspapers and skylights create a feeling of stepping into some bright young thing's fashionable Bankside loft.

Older traditions survive in this oldest part of London. The **Borough Café** (11 Park Street, tel: 7407 5048) is a 40-year-old veteran serving a breakfast menu of eggs, bacon, tomato and bubble-and-squeak to the Borough Market barrow boys from 4am. It's real London at real prices – increasingly hard to find. Almost next door is **Petit Robert** (tel: 7357 7003), a tiny spot whose presentation and decor feel like an old-fashioned Parisian bistro. Food is French, too, although fairly fussy and quite pricey; best to opt for the *prix-fixe* menu than order à la carte.

Another old-style eatery is smack by London Bridge station: **La Spezia** (tel: 7407 0277) has faded walls and a slightly weary air, but its Italian dishes are authentic if unexceptional and the wine list enterprising – Il Vino di Una Notte 97, a rosé from the Lake Garda area, translates as 'the wine of one special night'.

Pool of London

Around Hay's Galleria

The culinary revolution hasn't reach here yet. **The Blue Olive** (tel: 7407 6001) on Tooley Street, opposite the galleria's entrance, calls itself New York Italian, although we could see nothing very New York about the battuta of veal with oven-roasted stuffed plum tomato on an Oporto reduction (whatever an 'Oporto reduction' is). The **Bella Pasta** is one of a chain, catering mainly to local office workers.

Inside the galleria, the branch of **Café Rouge** gains unusual style from the soaring steel-and-glass eaves; its tables placed café-style on the pavement are helped by the fact that, since this is England, the eaves shelter diners from the rain. The menu's Gallic staples are augmented by French rural cheeses. The galleria branch of **Balls Brothers** ('wine merchants to the City gentry for five generations') focuses as much on eating as on drinking; inside its subterranean depths a series of seafood specialities can be ordered, and there's a champagne and oyster festival in September.

The galleria's prime waterfront spot has changed hands several times, as if the cuisine can't live up to the location, with river views of boats and *HMS Belfast* on the horizon. The current contender is **Kwan Thai** (tel: 7403 7373), a stylish blue-and-white affair that's calm and relaxing; try the good-value set menu for a taste test of Thai foods.

The otherwise dull stretch of Tooley Street between Hay's Galleria and Tower Bridge is enlivened by two little-known restaurants. **The Great Wall** (tel: 7357 0200) is a surprisingly pretty, delicate place, poorly located on the corner of a junction roaring with traffic. Inside, the spacious feeling is that of old-world Colonial; Peking, Cantonese and Szechuan is the fare.

'A nice place to meet/a nice place to eat' is the claim of **Fina Estampa** (tel: 7403 1342) – and London's only Peruvian restaurant, run by a husband and wife (he's British; she's Peruvian) lives up to the claim. The ambience is reminiscent of a colourful living room whose occupants happen to serve some of the most exotic dishes in town: starters such as *papa a la huancaina* (fromage frais sauce with Peruvian chillis over potatoes); mains such as *carapulcia* (dried potatoes Inca-style with pork and chicken and served with yuca). This restaurant provides home cooking in a down-home atmosphere and, though not cheap, is good value.

Butlers Wharf

One of the best London dining experiences is to sit outdoors on a soft summer night gazing at Tower Bridge illuminated in the moonlight. Four Butlers Wharf restaurants all in a row offer this view, with food and price ranges to suit each pocket. If the weather is foul or you arrive in the bleak midwinter, however, the experience quickly

Above: the cathedral-like Hays Galleria

deteriorates as the interiors of these restaurants are cramped and narrow.

Sophisticated, glamorous and romantic, the establishment that rises most elegantly to the occasion is **Le Pont de la Tour** (tel: 7403 8403, booking essential). This is the place that the Blairs took the Clintons when they visited – Pont de la Tour is the closest London gets to the chic open-air eating experience that Paris does so effortlessly. The food is classic Terence Conran fare: starters like lobster mayonnaise, main courses like

pan-fried sea bass with a tomato and red onion salsa. The wine list is long and excellent; the service smooth and non-obsequious, the tablecloths and crystal first-rate. Wildly expensive, but hey – what price dreams? *Top tip:* when booking, request an outdoor table and plan your evening around availability – the later the better, as most people will have left the wharf and too many passing tourists dampens the ardour.

Cantina del Ponte (tel: 7403 5403, booking advised) is the Conran next door, with a younger clientele and lower prices, but still far from cheap. Food is modern Italian like pumpkin and sage ravioli, with a few Mediterranean and Middle Eastern flourishes (lentils, aubergine) thrown in for good measure.

The other Butlers Wharf venues are two inexpensive chain restaurants, **All Bar One** and **ASK**, both good for pasta and both with spacious – if busy – terraces out front..

A little way downstream is Terence Conran's **Blue Print Café** (tel: 7378 7031, booking essential), a more intimate riverside experience than the gastrodomes already mentioned. Pretty blue-and-white steps (very Blue Print) on the river side of the Design Museum lead to an attractive, smallish L-shaped room on the first floor. Dining is

either indoors in winter, with the river attractively framed by windows, or on good days, out on the terrace but away from the hubbub of the tourists below. Prices are high but the food is good: daily changing dishes like spiced roast aubergine with coriander chutney to start, and roast cod with spiced lentils to follow. The Blue Print is many people's favourite Conran restaurant, although the **Butlers Wharf Chop House** (tel: 7403 3403, booking advised) also has its devotees. Flying the flag, Conran presents the best of British food using only the finest local produce: fish and chips, roast beef, smoked salmon, plus inventive vegetable dishes. On hot summer days, tables are placed outside next to the river and the gastrodomes. Be warned: patriotism does not come cheap. *Top tip:* order from the bar menu, where similar food is served at highly reduced prices.

Alternatively, you could try **The Apprentice** (tel: 7234 0254, booking advised) across the street, where the Terence Conran Butlers Wharf Chef School teaches its trainees. It's open for around two hours at lunchtime and two hours in the evening Mon–Fri (closed weekends). The atmosphere can be a little clinical but the food is tasty and a fraction of the normal Conran cost. *A la carte* is pricier than the set menus, but better.

The few non-Conran restaurants around Tower Bridge include a couple of pizza parlours, pub/wine bars serving lunchtime food,

and a scattering of nondescript Italian and Italian places. Worth singling out are the **Bengal Clipper** (tel: 7357 9001), an upscale Indian with nautical theme and Bengali and Goan traditions, and the **Circle Bar** (tel: 7407 1122) on Queen Elizabeth Street, essentially a bar for residents from the Circle apartment block, but with a decent brasserie menu.

Top: fine dining at Pont de la Tour
Right: another classic Conran restaurant

PUBS

In Chaucer's 14th-century *Canterbury Tales*, the Miller apologises in advance: 'And if the words get muddled in my tale, Just put it down to too much Southwark ale.' Sobriety has never been a characteristic of this area, which still has an extraordinary number of pubs. They're fairly staid today, though, compared to the taverns portrayed by Shakespeare or the drinking houses that gave birth to the 19th-century music hall.

Our selection here is far from comprehensive but includes the pubs with the best history, ambience and beers, as well as some more contemporary 'lifestyle' bars.

The South Bank

Underground: Southwark or Waterloo, unless otherwise stated

Doggett's
1 Blackfriar's Bridge
A modern pub by the Thames, giving a view of the river from the bar, but with a pointless area of seating on the walkway below with a towering wall concealing the sights. There is a larger beer garden at the rear of the building. Tourists and 'suits' form the bulk of business in a nice bar with dark wood and loads of gilt mirrors. There's pub grub, a function room, and children are welcome. Thomas Doggett was an actor who in 1715 donated a prize (Doggett's coat and badge) to the winner of a rowing race for Thames watermen between London Bridge and Chelsea; the race is still run annually.

Founder's Arms
52 Hopton Street
Underground: Southwark, London Bridge or Blackfriars
Built in the 1970s, the Founder's hasn't got architecture to swoon over, but the seating is conducive to lolling around, and the views more than make up for the frankly dull exterior. One whole side of the pub is glazed – perfect for admiring St Paul's, the City, the Millennium Bridge and Tate Modern. It's so busy you could be looking at a 20-minute wait (as we did) before service. There's a large outdoor patio if you can manage to nab a seat, and a good range of superior pub grub at reasonable prices make this a popular choice for office workers and tourists. Children can sit outside.

The Hogshead
52–4 Stamford Street
Spacious, modern pub with plenty of light wood and light, and some outside seating. The friendly staff are on hand to guide the office workers (daytime) and students (evenings) round the five regular and 10 guest ales per month, along with a selection of lagers and wines. The building was once a bank and the original safe in the cellar is used as the spirit store. There's good music behind the bar, a fair choice of pub grub, cheap, cheap prices and children are allowed in during the day. Closed at weekends.

The Jubilee Inn
79 York Road
Situated behind the London Eye, this typical local (patterned carpet and red velour seating) is in fact slightly different from your usual boozer. The Jubilee is gay-friendly, though not gay-exclusive. There's seating outside, a function room, pub grub, and children are welcome. Very friendly place, and we just loved the scarlet pool table.

The King's Arms
25 Roupell Street
A great side-street pub with conservation status serving the local community, suits and a sprinkling of actors. There's two bars and a lovely conservatory at the rear, which is dark and cosy in winter with a roaring fire, long wooden tables, candles and plants, and

Above: a pub sign proclaims a long tradition
Right: a drink outdoors, despite the Blackfriars Road traffic

light and airy in the summer thanks to the glazed roof. A friendly atmosphere permeates the place, helped along by up-tempo music, and amicable staff who will direct you to the real ales (four permanent and one guest) or the range of wines to enjoy with the tasty pub grub. Children are welcome until 7pm.

The Mulberry Bush
89 Upper Ground

Roomy, light-wood local with a frontage that opens fully onto the street, a bright family room/conservatory and a bistro with waitress service upstairs. When we visited, the Dorchester Gladiators over-40s rugby team (fresh from losing 61–17 to Romania's top club due to a mix-up, and shown on live TV over there) were singing at full throttle. Bar snacks are available, there's satellite TV, and the bistro doubles as a function room.

Paper Moon
24 Blackfriars Road

Pleasant, open-fronted (in the summer) pub, with local and office patronage. Reasonably priced pub grub, three real ales and specialist draught lagers, seating outside on the main road, and a small function room upstairs. Child-friendly.

Rose and Crown
47 Colombo Street

A Shepherd Neame (a 302-year-old brewery) recently refurbished corner pub. This is a laid-back place to while away a few hours, feeling at home among the regulars (of the office ilk) while supping one of five toothsome ales or two house lagers. The walls are covered in old sepia tints of Bankside, or you can read the beams: "An alcoholic is someone who drinks as much as you do, who you don't like" – Dylan Thomas. The staff are really friendly, there's posh pub grub weekday lunchtimes, a function room and a proper garden (it's a lawn) in which to catch a few rays while quaffing your brew. Open usual hours Mon–Fri plus Sat afternoons. Child-free.

The Stamford Arms
62 Stamford Street

Dark pub with nooks and crannies aplenty, lots of wood, brass and mirrors. Real ales on tap, and a selection of wines (the pub does wine promotion evenings once a month) for the office workers who frequent the place. There are also quiz nights and karaoke to keep the punters amused. There's a small seating area out front, posh pub grub and a function room. A child-free zone.

Studio Six
56 Upper Ground

Trendy hang-out in Gabriel's Wharf, with large scrubbed pine tables, an airy feel and funky music. The bar's name was inspired by the adjacent London Weekend Television headquarters – it has five studios and its staff gravitate to this one after work. There's a fine choice of beers and wines,

and above-average European cuisine. The staff are run ragged with the throngs of office boys, media girls, and hordes of tourists. Outside seating is on benches and tables reminiscent of a canteen when the weather permits. Children are welcome.

The Wellington
81–83 Waterloo Road

Big pub with big murals (of the Battle of Waterloo, of course, which may not amuse French visitors arriving by Eurostar), and accommodation upstairs if it all gets too much. There are five ales to choose from, good sandwiches among other pub grub, and it's always busy with office workers and rucksacked students. Children welcome at weekends during the day only.

The White Hart
29 Cornwall Road

Unpretentious local pub with comfy sofas and a large central bar. A mix of office workers and locals can enjoy camembert salad, or ciabatta with Mediterranean salad and brie, among other posh fare. There's benches on the street out front, and children are welcome.

The Windmill
86 The Cut

The Windmill has had a makeover, replacing celebrity portraits of stars from the nearby Old and Young Vic theatres with bright, light modernity. Ushers and Courage on tap, an outdoor seating area, and Thai food at reasonable prices. Child-friendly.

Bankside

Underground: London Bridge or Borough, unless otherwise stated

The Anchor
34 Park Street

The Anchor is full of quirky character, with a maze of odd rooms, dark staircases, brick hearths, hefty beams and creaking floorboards *(for its history, see pages 45–6)*. The features are authentic and make a visit here genuinely atmospheric. Customers are mainly office workers and tourists. The riverside terrace is mobbed in summer and has fantastic views of St Paul's, and there's a walled courtyard. Upstairs, the dining room is a great place to view London's skyline, and the food here is very good. Child-friendly.

Barrow Boy and Banker
6–8 Borough High Street

Sitting right by London Bridge, with Southwark Cathedral just behind, this is a huge pub with black-and-white tiled flooring, gorgeous oak panelling and a grand spiral staircase of marble and wrought iron dominating proceedings. If you can tear your eyes away from the chandeliers, oil paintings, etched glass, high ceilings and enormous portal, you'll find three permanent real ales plus one guest ale, above-average pub grub and a mix of bankers (the building was once a financial institution) and tourists – but not a barrow boy in sight. Closed at weekends. Child-friendly.

Belushi's
161 Borough High Street

Lively bar connected with the St Christopher's Inn hostels, with movie and musical memorabilia, modern furniture, big-screen television and loudish music. Customers – hostellers and office workers – may sit at tables on a raised platform on the street front with a cold bottle of lager. The food ranges from tasty to underwhelming, with burgers the best bet. There's comedy on Monday, live bands on Thursday and a DJ on Friday. It's happy hour all night Tuesday, and from 5–7pm Mon and Wed–Fri. Open 11am–11pm Mon–Wed, 11am–midnight Thur and Sat, 11am–12.30pm Fri, noon–10.30pm Sun. Child-free.

Left: a new style in Borough High Street

Blue Eyed Maid

173 Borough High Street

Long narrow haunt of office workers that has been trading for more than 300 years. There's wood aplenty, with heavy tables and high-backed settles. A larger-than-average range of wines is available, and the food is better than the usual pub fare. There's a large airy bar upstairs for private parties and al fresco seating in the alleyway adjacent. Closed weekends. Children not admitted.

Boot and Flogger

10–20 Redcross Way

Wine bar with an air of quiet comfort and exclusivity. Its name refers to a simple corking device. There are dishes of unshelled walnuts and green olives on the bar, and blackboards crammed with handwritten lists of ports and madeiras, wines and sherries. Leather armchairs and working wine barrels add to the atmosphere. Traditional food. You can start a tab on production of a credit card. Thanks to a charter dating to 1567, it could stay open round the clock, but sadly its largely business clientele confines it to Mon–Fri 11am–8pm. Children admitted.

Bunch of Grapes

2 St Thomas Street.

A bright, welcoming pub with primrose-painted brick walls and wooden floorboards spread with lovely worn rugs. Friendly staff serve up two Young's ales and a good choice of wines, and there's pub grub both at lunchtime and in the evening. There's a higgledy-piggledy garden at the back, with lush boughs overhanging the walls, and seating in the street out front. A good mix of locals, office and hospital staff, and tourists hang out here. Usual hours Mon–Fri, Sat noon– 5pm. Children not permitted.

The Charles Dickens

160 Union Street

A gem of a pub hidden down a dreary street linking Blackfriars Road and Southwark Bridge Road, with a buzzing, welcoming atmosphere, and sturdy wood tables throughout. The ambience is enhanced by sophisticated jazz music playing to an interesting crowd composed mainly of locals. Two real ales – one strong, one weaker – are served up, along with Guinness. There's a very small outdoor area, good staff, and the food is first-rate with doorstep sandwiches, hot meals, and delicious roasts on Sundays. Children are welcome on Sundays only. Live music on the last Friday of the month and quiz/karaoke nights alternate Thursdays.

The George Inn

77 Borough High Street

London's only remaining galleried coaching inn is now owned by the National Trust, though operated by the Whitbread brewery *(see page 57)*. Built in 1676, although a tavern of some sort has occupied the site since

Above: old-style service at the Boot and Flogger

1554, the George is a succession of inter-connecting nooks and crannies, with stone-flagged floors, plaster walls and large fireplaces. Charles Dickens mentions the pub in *Little Dorritt* and, because of his prodigious drinking coupled with lack of funds, he was forced to forfeit his life insurance policy to the landlord here. There's a good range of cask-conditioned guest ales for the huge volume of customers (tourists and office types) who may elect to sit outside in the large courtyard (even during inclement weather – there are outdoor heaters). Pub grub is served at the bar, or there's quality food in the restaurant (mainly British cuisine). The crowds can make service slow. Music-free and child-friendly.

Hop Cellars
24 Southwark Street

Stone-floored Balls Brothers wine bar that occupies the cellars of the elegant 19th-century Hop Exchange. Below this, there are a further couple of floors running the length of the building that once housed reprobates for nearby Clink Prison. The wine bar is frequented almost exclusively by (chiefly more mature) office staff, who have a choice of more than 90 wines, many by the glass. The tasty bar menu overlaps with the restaurant menu but is cheaper. There are Blind Tasting and Call My Bluff wine evenings. Open 11.30am–10pm Mon–Fri, closed weekends. The bar is child-friendly.

Above: historic galleries at the George Inn
Right: Henry VIII remembered

The King's Head
65 Newcommen Street

Side street pub refurbished pretty accurately to its former Victorian style, with lovely William Morris-type wallpaper. A crest affixed to the facade is from the original wooden London Bridge, which is why you'll see people gawping outside the pub while you're enjoying your drink at a comfortable table within. Food at lunchtime. Child-free.

The Market Porter
9 Stoney Street

Historic pub famous for opening its doors from 6am to 8.30am, ostensibly for market workers – although there's always a gaggle of post-ravers and other stragglers who fancy (or need) a jar. During normal hours, the clientele broadens. There's a fantastic choice of between 15 and 25 real ales a week and a range of posh pub grub if you can get past the hordes, the fug, and the stuffed animals that adorn the place. Children not welcome.

Old King's Head
King's Head Yard, Borough High Street
Situated down a quaint alleyway opposite the junction of Southwark Street and Borough High Street, this typical local, established in 1881, has dark wooden tables and stained-glass windows. During the week, office workers and staff from nearby Guy's Hospital can sample a big range of real ales; locals and tourists head here at the weekend. Happy hour (4–7pm) sees prices dropping to around £1.70 a pint. There's a small outside area and good-value traditional pub grub. Children are welcome lunchtimes in the upstairs area.

Old Thameside Inn
Pickfords Wharf, 1 Clink Street
An old riverside nutmeg warehouse spruced up with an excess of dark wood and brass. There's a range of ales and lagers for the tourists and office workers who crowd the pub at all hours, especially in summer when the outside decking by the river is heaving. There's a range of home-cooked food, and children are (kind of) welcome.

St Christopher's Inn
121 Borough High Street
A 16th-century Grade I listed building housing a boozer with a twist. Upstairs there's a purpose-built hostel with a cyber-café and sun terrace, both of which appeal to backpackers. The pub is long, dark and narrow, often with a bottleneck of traffic attempting to reach the pool table at the rear, where it's more spacious. Popular with staff from Guy's Hospital, locals and the ever-present youth from upstairs, who all take advantage of the late licence. Games nights, discos, good pub grub, a function room and big-screen TV. Children not allowed. Open Mon–Thur 11am–midnight, Fri–Sat 11–2am, Sun noon–10.30pm.

Slug and Lettuce
32–4 Borough High Street
Part of a chain, this large, light pub with parquet flooring, squashy sofas and low tables is a bar with pretentions aimed at 20- and 30-somethings. The building used to be a bank, though you'd not discern that from the decor. Customers are mainly office staff,

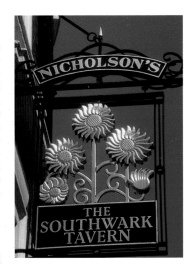

with students at weekends. The food is lovely but expensive. There's London Pride and Adnams on tap, plenty of wines, and it's child-friendly till 8pm, when presumably they're turfed out.

The Southwark Tavern
22 Southwark Street
The present building dates from 1857, but the downstairs bar contains holding cells for the Clink Prison which date from the 17th century, when Daniel Defoe was among the inmates. The Debtor's Bar, as it's named, can be rented for functions. Customers are office workers, hospital staff and a few tourists. There are three real ales – two of which change every couple of days – pub grub at lunchtimes and a few benches outside for when the weather turns pleasant.

The Wheatsheaf
6 Stoney Street
A Grade II listed building and local cockney boozer with two bars decked out in thickly varnished wood, with shiny red tables and prints of early 20th-century London. Customers, comprising (mostly male) office workers and (all male) construction staff, can enjoy a game of darts, choose dishes from the typical pub menu, and taste one of at least five carefully tended real ales, which the landlord changes on a daily basis. There's a tiny area out back for al fresco drinking. Children welcome.

Above: a pub with its own cells

Pool of London

Underground: London Bridge,
unless otherwise stated

Anchor Tap

20A Horsleydown Lane
Underground: Tower Hill
Built in the 1700s, this is a dark labyrinthine pub with a number of rooms, one given over to a pool table, another to a bank of fruit machines, a pinball machine and a dartboard, and three more for less strenuous pursuits. Built for midgets – the door frames are less than 5 ft (1.5 metres) high; you're guaranteed to bash your head after a few too many. Patronised by a healthy mix of locals, suits and the odd stray tourist. A ghostly horse and a couple of kids are said to run through the corridors upstairs, unsettling the barmaids. The beer garden is large, comfortable and flowery, but not twee. Low prices for London, a diverse range of pub grub, and a function room upstairs with an ornate fireplace. Child-friendly.

The Cooperage

48–50 Tooley Street
Creaky pub under railway arches with brick walls, sawdust on the floorboards, dusty bottles adorning every crevice and old lamps strung from the beams. There are a couple of home beers (Davy's Old Wallop and Davy's Ordinary) and an extensive wine list. The dining room at the rear of the building serves a nice choice of dishes, there's a function suite, and children are allowed in the back room. Customers tend to be from nearby offices. Open Mon–Tues 11am–9pm, Wed–Fri 11am–11pm, closed weekends.

Cynthia's Bridge Bar and Lounge

4 Tooley Street
Kitsch bar with a maze of mirrored, stainless-steel rooms and tiny pulsating red lights. After having a cocktail, such as Alien Vomit, mixed and served up by one of the robots, disorientation tends to set in. There are plenty of bottled beers to choose from, although humans serve these. The restaurant has good inexpensive food, and there's a selection of bar snacks. The whole place can be hired for groovy functions, there are club nights, and the staff are great. Open noon–11pm Mon–Wed, noon–1.30am Thur–Sat, noon–10.30pm Sun. Child-free.

The Elusive Camel

186 Tooley Street
Newish pub with a central bar and large windows. The old fittings have been cleverly revamped with fancy tilework and a marble fireplace left intact. There's a few benches outside where, if you crane your neck, you can see Tower Bridge. The menu includes wild boar-and-apple sausages with horseradish mash, and pretentious wording – check out 'elusive salad' and 'rustic bread'. Prices are pretty good, though. Fuller's London Pride and a range of lagers are on tap for the office folk and tourists. Child-free.

The Horniman at Hay's

Hay's Galleria, Tooley Street
Large gleaming pub with modern fittings made to look old. Americans are supposed to love its authenticity. There's a mezzanine, where food is served up, a sports bar downstairs, and comfy seating all round. Always busy with tourists and office workers, who can quaff any of eight real ales, or a range of special beers. Outside seating is never plentiful enough for thirsty punters, who perch on every available surface to enjoy the views of Tower Bridge, partially obscured by *HMS Belfast*, and the City. There's pub grub, and children are welcome.

Skinkers

42 Tooley Street
A cavernous wine bar underneath the railway arches of London Bridge station. It's old, massive, with an impressive restaurant full of dark red leather chesterfields, candles and polished dark wood, and lots of recesses for intimate conversations. Bar snacks are available. The place is popular with office staff, children can sit through the back, and there are Wine and Wisdom Fun Quiz evenings. Open Mon–Thur 11am–9pm, 11am–11pm Fri, closed weekends.

A Camel can go without a drink for 8 days – but who wants to be a Camel

Above: new-style bar with a trendy name
Right: old-style pub with its own ghosts

ANCHOR TAP

Practical Information

TRAVEL ESSENTIALS

Public Transport

The Jubilee Line stops at Waterloo, Southwark and London Bridge, and the City branch of the Northern Line at London Bridge and Borough. The District and Circle Lines have stops on the north side of the river at Blackfriars, Monument and Tower Hill and the Central Line at St Paul's and Bank (for Monument); on a fine day, walking from these stations across the various Thames bridges is a visually dramatic way of approaching Southwark and the South Bank.

Many buses serve the area. To Blackfriars Bridge: 45, 63, 172. To Southwark Bridge: 149. To London Bridge: 17, 21, 22A, 35, 40, 43, 47, 48, 133, 344, 501, 521, P3, P11, D1, X43. To Tooley Street: 47, P11. To Southwark Street: 149, 344, D1, P11. To Borough High Street: 21, 35, 40, 133, P3. To Tower Bridge: 42, 78, 188.

For Underground and bus information, tel: 7222 1234.

Cycling

Cycle routes in Southwark link the riverside attractions with green areas such as Dulwich Village. For a *Cycling in Southwark* map, tel: 7525 5474, or visit the Southwark Cyclists' website: info@southwarkcyclists. org.uk. The London Bicycle Tour Company at 1A Gabriel's Wharf on the South Bank (tel: 7928 6838) rents out all kinds of bikes (including a bicycle rickshaw) as well as roller blades. Cycle hire is also available from On Your Bike at 52–54 Tooley Street (tel: 7378 6669). A popular cycle retailer is Evans UK at 77–79 The Cut (tel: 7928 4785).

Car Parks

There are several car parks along the South Bank, including one in the National Theatre's basement. There are smaller car parks along Union Street and Southwark Street, but most spaces are snapped up by local office workers. On-street parking is comparatively scarce and parking meters are rigorously policed by traffic wardens.

EMERGENCIES

For fire, police and ambulances, dial 999. **St Thomas' Hospital** (tel: 7928 9292) has a 24-hour accident and emergency service. Its entrance is on Lambeth Palace Road, to the west of Westminster Bridge.

TOURIST INFORMATION

Southwark Information Centre

The Southwark Information Centre is a handy starting point for visits to the Pool of London, Bankside and the South Bank. It's easily identified by the 'Southwark Needle', a 52-ft (16-metre) stone obelisk inclined at an angle of 19.5° and standing outside it on the southeast corner of London Bridge.

Multilingual staff can provide advice, directions, leaflets, and details of venues. There's a selection of guidebooks, maps, gifts and souvenirs, plus a currency exchange and a booking service for accommodation, theatre and events.

The Centre is open from 10am–6pm, Mon–Sat and 11am–6pm Sun, Easter–Oct. Winter hours are 10am–4pm Mon–Sat and 11am–4pm Sun. For Southwark-related enquiries only, tel: 7403 8299. Email: info@southwark-online.co.uk. The website address is www.southwark-online.co.uk.

TOURS

River Trips

A number of boat services operate along the River Thames from this area. The City Cruises' Millennium Express goes between Waterloo Millennium Pier and Greenwich via Blackfriars (tel: 7740 0400, www.city-cruises.com). Frequent services also operate from Westminster Pier on the north side of

Left: Southwark Underground station

the river. The Central London River Hopper is a Canary Wharf–Rotherhithe Holiday Inn–London Bridge Pier–Blackfriars commuter shuttle running during rush hours only, Mon–Fri except public holidays (tel: 01793-433600, www.whitehorse.co.uk).

Guided Tours

Southwark Tour Guides Association (tel: 7231 5988) runs themed walks (e.g. seafaring traditions, historic theatres) and can organise days out for coach parties. London Walks (7624 3978) has a Monday annd Saturday morning tour of 'Shakespeare's London', starting at Westminster Station and taking a boat across the river.

Also in the Borough of Southwark...

Although outside the area covered by this book, England's oldest purpose-built art gallery, the **Dulwich Picture Gallery** (12-minute rail journey from Victoria Station to West Dulwich; tel: 8693 5254) is well worth a visit. Housed in a magnificent 1811 building designed by Sir John Soane, it contains a superb collection of 17th- and 18th-century European masterpieces, including Rubens, Rembrandt, Reynolds and Caneletto. Its website is: dulwichpicturegallery.org.uk.

The council-owned **South London Gallery** (65 Peckham Road, tel: 7703 6120) is a leading venue for contemporary art exhibitions and has a permanent display of 19th- and 20th-century British artists.

Bermondsey Antiques Market (early Fri mornings, Bermondsey Square, off Tower Bridge Road) has 500 traders. Also known as Caledonian Market. Best items go by 10am.

NIGHTLIFE

Most nightlife is based in bars and pubs. The one renowned dance club is the **Ministry of Sound** (103 Gaunt Street, tel: 7378 6528), London's top house-music venue.

Apart from the Royal National Theatre, the Old Vic, Young Vic and Shakespeare's Globe (covered in the main text), the 90-seater **Southwark Playhouse**, housed in a Victorian warehouse at 62 Southwark Bridge Road (tel: 7620 3494) and the small **Union Theatre** in Union Street (tel: 7261 9876) have a varied repertoire of plays and events.

ACCOMMODATION

All the hotel prices quoted below include value-added tax.

Days Inn

54 Kennington Road, SE1
Underground: Lambeth North
Tel: 7922 1331, fax: 7922 1441
waterloo@premierhotels.co.uk
www.daysinn.com/london12578
Cost of double room only: £69.50.
Close to the Imperial War Museum and a short stroll from Tate Modern, this new six-floor hotel, part of an American chain, has lots of amenities. 162 rooms.

Holiday Inn Express

103–109 Southwark Street, SE1
Underground: Blackfriars
Tel: 7401 2525, fax: 7401 3322
stay@expresssouthwark.co.uk
Cost of a double room with breakfast: £87.
Close to Blackfriars Bridge and Tate Modern, this chain hotel with helpful staff has 90 modern rooms and is good value for money.

Holiday Inn Nelson Dock

265 Rotherhithe Street, SE16
Docklands Light Railway: Canada Water
Tel: 7231 1001, fax: 7231 0599
reservations@holidayinnnd.co.uk
www.holidayinnnd.co.uk
Cost of a double room only: £99–£157.
Opposite Canary Wharf, this hotel with 368 large, airy rooms has its own courtesy river taxi to ferry you to the main landing stages along the Thames, as well as a bus to take you to the nearest DLR station.

London Bridge Hotel

8–18 London Bridge Street, SE1
Underground: London Bridge
Tel: 7855 2200, fax: 7855 2233
reservations@london-bridge-hotel.co.uk
www.london-bridge-hotel.co.uk
Cost of a double room only: £170.
This recently built, modern hotel is located opposite London Bridge station. The 138 rooms over seven floors are comfortable and well-appointed. The public areas are tastefully furnished and the hotel has its own pub, as well as a Simply Nico restaurant.

Mercure London City Bankside

75–79 Southwark Street, SE1
Underground: Southwark
Tel: 7902 0800, fax: 7902 0810
h2814@accor-hotels.com
www.mercure.com
Cost of a double room only: £145.
This newly opened French chain hotel is close to Tate Modern and the Globe Theatre. The hotel has business facilities, a bar, a gym and its own restaurant, The Loft, with a range of reasonably priced wines. The 100 rooms are decorated in plain, contemporary style and have plenty of features.

London County Hall Travel Inn

Belvedere Road, SE1
Underground: Waterloo or Westminster
Tel: 7902 1600, fax: 7902 1619
www.travelinn.co.uk
Cost for a double room only: £64.95.
Large, budget chain hotel in a prime, central location (it occupies part of the former County Hall building) beside the Thames but with no view of it. The 313 spacious rooms all have en suite facilities and two fold-out beds for children, making it one of the best-value hotels in London – so it's heavily booked.

London Marriott County Hall Hotel

County Hall, Belvedere Road, SE1
Underground: Waterloo or Westminster
Tel: 7928 5200, fax: 7928 5300
www.marriotthotels.com/LONCH
Cost of a double room without breakfast: £235–£255, lower weekend rates.
Occupying the other part of the former County Hall, this 200-room hotel offers stunning views of Big Ben and the Thames from the more expensive rooms. Probably the only hotel in London with sharks in the basement (it's built above the London Aquarium). There are lots of amenities, including a leisure club with an indoor pool.

The Mad Hatter

3-7 Stamford Street, SE1
Underground: Waterloo or Blackfriars
Tel: 7401 9222, fax: 7401 7111
madhatter@fullers.demon.co.uk
www.fullers.co.uk/retail/hotels/hatter.html
Cost of a double room without breakfast: £82.50, lower weekend rates.

Housed in a former hat factory near Blackfriars Bridge, this small, neat hotel has 30 spacious rooms with en suite facilities. Its restaurant serves up decent pub grub.

Novotel Waterloo

113 Lambeth Road, SE1
Underground: Waterloo or Lambeth North
Tel: 7793 1010, fax: 7793 0202
www.novotel.com
Cost of a double room only: £145.
Opened in 1995, this French-owned hotel faces Lambeth Palace, with the Houses of Parliament and Westminster Abbey on the opposite bank of the Thames. There are 187 rooms with plenty of facilities.

Thistle Tower Hotel

St Katharine's Way, E1
Underground: Tower Hill
Tel: 7481 2575, fax: 7488 4106
www.thistlehotels.com
Cost of a double room only: £185.
What this huge (801 rooms), modern hotel lacks in charm is compensated for by its riverside location close to the Tower of London, Tower Bridge and St Katharine's Dock. It's a brisk five-minute walk to the nearest Tube station, a handy choice for businessmen who want to be near the City.

Tower Bridge Travel Inn Capital

Tower Bridge Road, SE1
Underground: London Bridge or Tower Hill
Tel: 7940 3700, fax: 7940 3719
www.travelinn.co.uk
Cost of a double room only: £64.95.
Great value in a good location close to Tower Bridge, this chain hotel has 195 rooms. The price covers two children sharing the room.

FURTHER READING

London Encyclopaedia, edited by Ben Weinreb and Christopher Hibbert (1987)
Medieval Southwark, Martha Carlin (1996)
Old Bankside, Grace Golden (1951)
Southwark: An Illustrated History, Leonard Reilly (1998)
Southwark at War, Rib Davis and Pam Schweitzer (1996)
The Story of Bankside, Mary Boast (1985)
The Story of 'The Borough', Mary Boast (1997)